CONTEMPORARY THEMES 1

The Fight for The Republic

SITARAM YECHURY

CONTEMPORARY THEMES 1

The Fight for The Republic

SITARAM YECHURY

INTRODUCTION BY **PRABHAT PATNAIK**

TULIKA BOOKS

SAHMAT

Published by
Tulika Books
44 (first floor), Shahpur Jat, New Delhi 110 049, India
www.tfortulika.com

in association with

Safdar Hashmi Memorial Trust (SAHMAT)
36 Pandit Ravi Shankar Shukla Lane, New Delhi 110 001, India

First edition (paperback), December 2024

ISBN: 978-81-979383-8-2

Printed at Chaman Offset, Delhi 110 002

Contents

7
Introduction PRABHAT PATNAIK

31
Pseudo-Hinduism Exposed

58
What Is Hindu Rashtra?

90
India at 75

Introduction

PRABHAT PATNAIK

Sitaram Yechury was a brilliant student of economics at the Jawaharlal Nehru University, Delhi, who abandoned his PhD research to become a full-time activist of the Communist Party of India (Marxist). The Communist movement has over the years drawn many academically brilliant persons to its ranks: Dr Gangadhar Adhikari's name comes readily to one's mind, whom Albert Einstein had gone to visit out of curiosity when Adhikari was a researcher at the Humboldt University in Berlin; so does the name of B.T. Ranadive whose Master's dissertation at Bombay University on India's population was published as an important book on the subject at the time; and of Rebati Mohan Barman who had stood first in the School Final Examinations in the whole of Bengal and also won a gold medal in his university days. Sitaram belonged to that lineage.

His academic training is evident in the essays in this book: there is in general a meticulous attempt to establish his propositions with proper references, and, on occasion, a scrupulous examination of other alternative hypotheses. Even though Sitaram was a senior leader of the Party when these essays were written, he does not resort to mere assertions, as is frequently the case, in making his points.

This is also in keeping with the underlying intellectual position of these essays. The one basic theme running through them is: reason versus unreason. The Hindutva forces' fomenting of hatred against a hapless religious minority is not just morally reprehensible; it is advanced on the basis of a perception of history which is contrary to all available evidence and consists only of assertions that are not even internally logically consistent. They are, in short, based on an invoking of unreason. As against this, what these essays promote, namely an inclusive nationalism that encompasses all religious, linguistic and ethnic groups, and sustains a secular democratic polity, is founded on a reading of our history that relies on evidence and reason. The conflict between inhumanity and humanity, therefore, is not a conflict between two alternative ideological perceptions of history; it is a conflict between a scientific and an ideological perception of history, between a perception based on evidence and one that has scant regard for evidence. In fact, one of Sitaram's major worries in these essays is that the Hindutva elements' attempt to control the education system and propagate their *weltanschauung* through it, would lead to a general destruction of reason in the country that would have a remarkably regressive effect on the country's academic standards and intellectual life.

Sitaram takes our anti-colonial struggle as a decisive period in the formation of our national consciousness.

Unlike European nationalism that came into being in the wake of the Westphalian peace treaties in the seventeenth century, and that invariably located an 'external enemy' within the country against whom the 'nation' had to be united (Bilgrami 2014), the anti-colonial nationalism in countries like India had an inclusive character; it sought to unite all segments of society against the colonial rulers. In contrast, both the Muslim League and the Hindutva ideologies represented a throwback to the post-Westphalian nationalism of Europe, in so far as each claimed to champion the interest of only one particular segment of the population to the exclusion of others; the colonial rulers encouraged such divisive ideologies, which ultimately resulted in the partition of the country. As against this, the *anti-colonial nationalism sought to unite everyone in a common struggle* on the basis of a vision which ultimately got enshrined in the Constitution, the vision of a secular democracy committed to social justice and federalism.

The Hindutva vision of a *Hindu Rashtra* is not just against the Constitution (and its votaries, no matter what they say, have scant respect for the Constitution), not just majoritarian, but in openly advocating a second-class status for the minorities, indubitably 'fascistic'.

Within the anti-colonial struggle itself, however, Sitaram emphasizes two distinct trends. While there was complete unity on the question of the secular-democratic and federal republic that was to succeed colonial rule, the Left strand saw the defence of its secular-democratic character as being dependent upon the pursuit of a development trajectory that would break asset concentration, especially land concentration, and take the country in a socialist direction. Since this strand could not acquire hegemony over the anti-colonial struggle by the time of independence, post-independence development took the form of the pursuit of a capitalist trajectory, and that too without breaking land concentration and without dealing the decisive blows against feudalism that capitalism in its classical phase had done in Europe, in the wake for instance of the French Revolution.

It is this which, Sitaram argues, enabled the Hindutva elements that had kept themselves scrupulously aloof from the colonial struggle, to sneak into the dominant position they currently occupy in the polity, despite the setback they had received owing to their complicity in Gandhiji's assassination, and despite their being rejected by the people at large who had rallied around the anti-colonial struggle. Even now, however, they do not enjoy the confidence of the majority of the people, and can be defeated if all patriotic forces – that is, forces loyal to the spirit of the anti-colonial struggle – unite against them.

II

These essays were not written with the objective of constituting a comprehensive book on the emergence of neo-fascism; they were written for specific occasions and hence each of them has only a specific objective. Taken as a whole, therefore, they leave certain gaps in our understanding of the *totality* of the current conjuncture.

I shall devote the rest of this Introduction to pointing out some of these gaps, and how one may fill them in a way that is in conformity with Sitaram's thinking. In fact, I feel confident that Sitaram would have more or less agreed with whatever is written below.

One remarkable aspect of the current conjuncture is that the ascendancy of neo-fascism is a *global phenomenon*. Neo-fascist forces have become powerful and even come to office in countries ranging from the United States to Brazil, Argentina, Hungary, Poland, Turkey, and even countries of Western Europe. While it is perfectly legitimate to see the absence of decisive blows against feudalism in India as providing a fertile ground for the neo-fascist upsurge here (as an attempt to usher in a counter-revolution against the prolonged but incomplete social revolution that had resulted from a social emancipation struggle accompanying the anti-colonial struggle as a parallel movement), its global reach has to be located in some additional phenomenon; and this phenomenon, clearly, is the crisis of neo-liberalism, which is why the ascendancy of neo-fascism characterizes not only a country like Germany that had not witnessed a thoroughgoing bourgeois revolution, unlike England and France, but these latter countries as well. In France in particular, Marine Le Pen's party has been very close to power; while it was thwarted in the recent French parliamentary elections by a coalition of the Left, its potency has been far from dented.

Put differently, everywhere in the world there is a collapse of the appeal of the liberal Centre (that straddles both conservative and social democratic formations); and the reason for it lies in the fact that in the popular perception this Centre has been closely identified with the neo-liberal economic regime, which brought hardships to the people when it was not in crisis, but even greater hardships when it is in crisis.

Thus, the phenomenon of neo-liberalism has to be brought into an analysis of neo-fascism to provide a complete picture. Within the post-independence development trajectory, in other words, we must distinguish between the *dirigiste* phase and the neo-liberal phase; and this is true not just for India but for the post-war capitalist world as a whole. In Europe the immediate post-war period saw Social Democratic governments adopting welfare state measures as part of Keynesian demand management, in order to bring down unemployment rates to historic lows; the US too brought down its unemployment rate officially to just 4 per cent in the Kennedy years, though the instrument used there was not welfare expenditure but armaments spending by the state (Baran and Sweezy 1966). India of course adopted planning, inspired by the Soviet experience, but only 'partial planning' because of the presence of a large private sector. *Dirigisme* was the pervasive economic arrangement of the post-war period, and it brought about what has been called the 'Golden Age of Capitalism'. This period also saw, through the process of centralization of capital, the emergence of an international finance capital, under whose pressure it gave way everywhere to a neo-liberal regime. Neo-liberalism has seen, even before it ran into a crisis, a remarkable slowing down of the growth rate of the world economy.

In India the opposite seems to have happened between the two periods: even though the GDP growth rate under *dirigisme* was much higher compared to the stagnation or retrogression of the colonial era, this growth rate seems to have risen substantially in the neo-liberal era that began in the mid-1980s here but gathered momentum from 1991 onwards. This contrast has been used to run down the *dirigiste* period, but we need to keep several points in mind while making a comparative assessment of the two periods, quite apart from the fact that the acceleration of the growth rate under neo-liberalism itself is highly contested.

The first thing to note is that there has been a dramatic increase in income inequality during the neo-liberal period. According to the World Inequality Lab, the share of the top 1 per cent of the population in national income, which had been 6 per cent in 1982, increased to 22.4 per cent in 2022–23, which is higher than at any time during the last one hundred years. This increase is so striking that it cannot be explained merely as arising from any statistical quirks associated with the method of calculation. What is more, this share had actually fallen during the *dirigiste* period to reach a low of just 6 per cent in 1982. While the *dirigiste* period, in other words, may have had a lower GDP growth rate, it entailed a move towards a more egalitarian society. Neo-liberalism has meant just the opposite: possibly a higher GDP growth rate but, associated with it, a sharp increase in income inequality that fundamentally undermines democracy.

It is not even the case that the benefits of growth have only been unequally distributed with *everyone* being better off than before. There is plenty of evidence to show that the degree of nutritional deprivation has actually increased; and if poverty is defined in terms of nutritional deprivation, then the relative magnitude of absolute poverty has increased. The proportion of the rural population that could not access 2200 calories per person per day (the benchmark used by the erstwhile Planning Commission for defining rural poverty) increased from 58 per cent in 1993–94 to 68 per cent in 2011–12. The proportion of the urban population that could not access 2100 calories per person per day (the benchmark for defining urban poverty by the old Planning Commission) increased over the same period from 57 to 65 per cent. The next National Sample Survey, undertaken in 2017–18, found that the per capita real consumption expenditure for the entire population in rural India had fallen in absolute terms by 9 per cent compared to 2011–12; the extent of rural poverty by the above criterion of calorie intake had exceeded 80 per cent, while urban poverty remained more or less unchanged (U. Patnaik, forthcoming). The *dirigiste* period had meant, in total contrast to the neo-liberal one, not only a reduction in income inequality as measured above, but also a stabilization or even a marginal decline in the extent of poverty.

Secondly, neo-liberalism has meant a slowing down

of the rate of job creation compared to *dirigisme*. There are several obvious reasons for it. One, the increase in income inequality, even assuming that the same proportion of income is consumed by the rich as by the poor, necessarily means a change in the pattern of demand. The rich tend to emulate the life-style of the western elite and this life-style is much less employment-intensive than that of the poor, so that a rise in income inequality tends to reduce the growth of labour demand. Two, since neo-liberalism entails relatively unrestricted flows of goods across country-borders, it intensifies competition between producers located in different countries; there is as a result a quickening of the pace of technological progress that tends to be essentially labour-displacing.

In fact the combined effects of these factors has been so great that the rate of job creation in the neo-liberal era is estimated to have fallen even below the natural rate of growth of the labour force, pushing the unemployment rate above what prevailed in the *dirigiste* era.

Thirdly, the increase in income inequality necessarily produces a tendency towards overproduction, as the propensity to consume of the poor is much higher than of the rich (Kalecki 1954). Since inequality has been increasing in every country and also globally, this tendency, kept in check for a while because of asset–price bubbles in the US that stimulate consumption through a wealth effect, finally burst upon the world economy after the collapse of the housing bubble in the US. The world economy thus has not only grown at a slower rate under neo-liberalism, even before it ran into a crisis, compared to the *dirigiste* era (which of course ended in different countries at different dates, but roughly in the 1970s and the 1980s), but it has also got engulfed of late in a crisis of stagnation.

This distinction between the *dirigiste* era and the neo-liberal era within capitalism is important. The crisis of neo-liberalism produces the immediate context for the growth of neo-fascism and accounts for its being a global phenomenon. Fascist elements exist in every modern society, but usually as fringe elements. They move centre stage when suddenly they get the financial and media support of monopoly capital – and they get this support in a period of crisis when monopoly capital perceives a threat to its hegemony; it then supports fascist or neo-fascist elements to promote an alternative discourse, one that foments hatred against a minority religious or linguistic or ethnic group. Such a discourse serves to divert attention away from problems of material conditions of life; it also divides the people, making it difficult for them to act unitedly to mount a challenge to the hegemony of monopoly capital. Besides, the unemployment associated with the crisis provides the fascist elements with plenty of opportunity to find recruits for their gangs of vigilante thugs.

India is no exception to this phenomenon: what we have is the 'othering' of a religious minority group and the coming into being of an alliance between the corporate–financial oligarchy that is integrated with international finance capital, on the one hand, and the *Hindutva* fascists, on the other.

All the features associated with classical fascism are visible here: a fomenting of hatred against a minority; an alliance between monopoly capital and the neo-fascists within which the latter become particularly close to a *new stratum* of monopolists;[1] the use of state power to repress all opponents and critics of the regime; the use of neo-fascist thugs to supplement state repression; and the promotion of a personality cult around the 'leader', criticism against whom is dubbed as constituting an anti-national act.

III

There is however a major difference between classical fascism and neo-fascism which is of fundamental importance. Classical fascism had come to power in the context of the crisis, but had also overcome the crisis by increasing the level of aggregate demand through larger government expenditure on armaments *financed by a fiscal deficit*. Japan was the first country to come out of the Great Depression in 1931 by building up its military might under a fascist regime; Germany followed suit shortly thereafter when Hitler came to power in 1933 and started building up Germany's military might. Both countries overcame the mass unemployment that had

---

[1] Fascism's close nexus with a new stratum of monopoly capital is a well-attested fact. See, for example, Guerin ([1939] 1973), for the case of Germany.

characterized them during the Depression; there was in fact a brief period when unemployment had disappeared but the horrors of the war had not yet appeared, when the fascist governments became quite popular in their respective countries.

Neo-fascism, however, is totally incapable of overcoming economic stagnation and the resulting unemployment. This is because for government expenditure to increase the level of aggregate demand, it mut be financed either by a fiscal deficit, or by taxes on the capitalists or the rich in general who save a part of their incomes. If government expenditure is financed by taxes on the working people who consume the bulk of their incomes, then it hardly adds to aggregate demand; it only changes the composition of aggregate demand, not its magnitude. But both these ways of financing government expenditure, namely by taxing the rich or enlarging the fiscal deficit, are disliked by *international* finance capital and are hence foreclosed for the government of the *nation-state*, which is constrained to respect the caprices of international finance capital for fear of otherwise triggering a damaging capital flight.

It is for this reason that larger government expenditure to enlarge aggregate demand as a way out of the crisis is not possible under neo-liberalism, even if the government could somehow ensure that the demand-increasing effect of such expenditure remained confined exclusively to domestic goods and did not 'leak out' abroad through larger imports.

This is where classical fascism was in a better

position. Finance capital was not international but national, so that the government of the nation-state could overcome its opposition to a fiscal deficit (which finance. incidentally, is always opposed to); in addition, the domestic economy could be protected to ensure that the multiplier effects of government spending remained confined within its domain. But with finance being globally mobile no government of a nation-state, whether it is a liberal bourgeois government or a neo-fascist government, can increase employment in the domestic economy. Overcoming the crisis, it follows, requires going beyond neo-liberalism. The crisis that is a product of neo-liberalism cannot be overcome within neo-liberalism.

For this reason, no neo-fascist government will ever be able to acquire the kind of popularity that the classical fascist governments could while undertaking war preparations and thereby increasing employment (before actual war broke out on a large scale); and the diversionary discourse provided by the neo-fascists will never be so successful that people in large numbers fall prey to it while ignoring their state of employment and, in general, their material conditions of life. Unless the neo-fascist regime completely does away with elections, which is not feasible in the current context, or rigs them successfully on a large scale, it is conceivable that it will be voted out on occasions, as has happened to Donald Trump in the US or to Jair Bolsonaro in Brazil. But even on such occasions, unless the liberal political formation that comes to power can take steps to improve the material conditions of life of the working people, above all their state of employment, which it can do only if it goes beyond the neo-liberal regime, it too will get voted out and the neo-fascists will come back to power.

This has very important implications for the fight against neo-fascism and for the defence of the secular-democratic nature of the republic, which is the theme of these essays by Sitaram.

IV

Immanent in classical fascism was the unleashing of war, as it came in a period of intense inter-imperialist rivalry; accordingly, it blew itself up in that war after having inflicted a great cost on humanity. Neo-fascism however is emerging in a period of the muting of inter-imperialist rivalry, arising from the fact that international finance capital wants the entire world as its area of operation and does not want it broken up into economic territories of rival powers. Neo-fascism, therefore, would neither blow itself up through war nor disappear as long as the crisis of neo-liberalism lasts, which in turn means as long as neo-liberalism itself lasts.

This is so for an additional reason as well. Walter Benjamin, the German philosopher, is reported to have held the view that fascism comes on the backs of a failed revolution.[2] He was of course thinking of the German experience, where there had been repeated attempts at a proletarian revolution following the Bolshevik

---

[2] While the original place where Benjamin said this remains obscure, this remark is often quoted by the Slovenian philosopher Slavoj Žižek.

revolution. The failure of these attempts had left the German proletariat exhausted and too weak to resist the ascendancy of fascism. While in countries like India there has been no repeat of the German experience of the inter-war years, the proletariat has got weakened by the introduction of the neo-liberal regime and its striking power greatly diminished, which no doubt has facilitated the rise of neo-fascism.

To put the matter differently, fascism or neo-fascism thrives in that twilight zone where the working people are not strong enough to resist its rise but not so weak as to allay monopoly capital's fears about their challenging its hegemony in a period of crisis. Neo-liberalism creates precisely that twilight zone.

Noe-liberalism weakens the working class in at least three distinct ways. The first is the fact that it gives rise to intensified competition between workers of different countries, as capital now becomes globalized while workers remain organized on national lines; it is for this reason that workers in the advanced countries see their wages stagnating or declining as they face competition from workers of the third world, where capital threatens to relocate if they demand higher wages. The second is the rise in the unemployment rate for reasons we have discussed earlier, which inevitably weakens the bargaining position of the workers and the strength of the trade union movement. The third is the privatization of public sector enterprises. All over the world a larger proportion of public sector workers are unionized compared to private sector workers: in the US, for instance, the ratios (including the sphere of education) are 33 per cent and 7 per cent, respectively; correspondingly, the striking power of workers is greater in the public sector than in the private sector. The privatization of public sector units therefore results generally in a weakening of the working class as a whole.

Neo-liberalism thus creates the conditions for neo-fascism both by weakening the working class (and the working people generally), and by necessarily precipitating a crisis of stagnation and unemployment from which there is no escape within it. It follows, then, that the unity of patriotic forces that Sitaram calls for in order to defend the secular democratic nature of our polity against the neo-fascist onslaught, must consciously aim at the same time to escape thraldom to the neo-liberal order that is the source of people's impoverishment and the base for neo-fascism.

An implicit awareness of this fact is already evident in India. The principal opposition party, the Congress, for instance, has come out with proposals for various welfare schemes, and the ruling Bharatiya Janata Party (BJP), despite pooh-poohing all such schemes as 'freebies', has also introduced some in the election season. The most prominent of these is the minimum income scheme whose objective is to ensure that everyone gets a minimum income, though its modalities remain to be worked out. Several economists too have mooted this idea of the government ensuring a basic minimum income for all.

The figures so far talked about in the context of this

scheme are very low; but even leaving that aside, there are three obvious problems with such a scheme. The first is that it appears in the nature of a largesse on the part of the state, which, no matter how helpful to the beneficiaries, is implicitly inimical to their dignity. The second is that it makes the scale of the transfers, and even the very continuance of the scheme, dependent on the fiscal situation faced by the government. There is no guarantee that funds for this scheme would constitute the first charge on the government's budget and will therefore be always forthcoming. The third problem is that cash transfers do not by any means necessarily mean a real improvement in people's lives. Cash transfers to a male head of a household will not always be used for the household's betterment; but even if this problem is overcome by making the transfers to a female member, the fact remains that children cannot go to school if there are no schools nearby, family members cannot go to a hospital if there are no hospitals nearby, and so on. Besides, private schools and hospitals jack up their fees if they know that there are such transfers, so that the transfers that appeared sufficient to start with, turn out not to be.

These problems do not arise if, instead of discretionary cash transfers, a set of constitutionally guaranteed, fundamental, justiciable economic rights for every citizen, on a par with the fundamental rights that currently exist in the Indian Constitution, is instituted. In fact, such a measure will also overcome the anomaly that currently exists within the Indian Constitution, where all economic proposals for building a just and egalitarian society are included within the Directive Principles of State Policy, which are not justiciable and can be violated with impunity.

Such fundamental economic rights will remove the provision of welfare to the people from the realm of largesse by the government, and confer upon them the dignity of citizenship. They will automatically make them the first charge on the budget; they will entail not the provision of cash but the building of requisite public institutions like schools and hospitals; and by removing 'targeting' altogether, they will eliminate conflicts over who should be included within the targeted beneficiaries.

V

Instituting such a set of fundamental economic rights is eminently feasible financially. Of course the mobilization of financial resources *per se* does not ensure the availability of the requisite real resources, and hence does not guarantee that implementing such a scheme will be non-inflationary. To avoid inflation, appropriate real resources must be made available in the economy, which would require an increase in output in particular sectors, notably in agriculture and especially of foodgrains. This, I believe, is perfectly feasible; but I shall confine myself here only to the question of financial resource mobilization.

Let us consider the institution of just five fundamental economic rights: a right to food (making available to everyone foodgrains exactly on the same terms as they were available for the below-poverty-line population before the pandemic); a right to employment (if a person does not get employment, then he or she must get a full wage); a right to free quality public education (at least up to the Higher Secondary level); a right to free quality public health care (through a National Health Service); and a right to a living non-contributory old age pension and disability benefit. Instituting these will cost, in addition to what is currently earmarked for these purposes under various heads, an additional 10 per cent of our GDP.

Taking into account the flowback in the form of tax revenue from any government spending, an additional expenditure of 10 per cent of GDP requires the mobilization of additional tax revenue of about 7 per cent of GDP. This additional tax revenue can be mobilized through the imposition of just two taxes on the top 1 per cent of the population: a wealth tax of 2 per cent, and an inheritance tax of one-third on whatever is passed on each year by this segment (Patnaik and Ghosh 2020).

These are extremely modest tax proposals, and that too only for levying on the top 1 per cent of the population. In the US, for example, both Bernie Sanders and Elizabeth Warren, who had entered the primaries in 2020 for getting the Democratic Party's presidential nomination, had proposals for far heavier wealth taxes than these. True, the wealth tax has virtually disappeared in India because it has yielded little revenue, but that suggests a lack of seriousness in implementing it rather than a lack of wisdom behind it.

Likewise, an inheritance tax in fact follows from the *defence* of the capitalist system: this states that capitalists have a certain special quality (whatever that may be) that justifies their getting an income category called profit; but then the progeny of the capitalists must display that same quality before they can claim any entitlement to profit. There must therefore be a level playing field with inherited wealth being heavily penalized; and on this level playing field whoever displays this capitalist quality should become a capitalist and be entitled to earn a profit. What is quite amazing is that India does not have any inheritance taxation (by contrast, a country like Japan has a 55 per cent rate of inheritance taxation, and the United States and the United Kingdom, 40 per cent); it is time this was rectified.

VI

Any welfare state measure that is more than mere tokenism will invite the wrath of globalized finance, for it will necessarily mean either a larger fiscal deficit or heavier taxes on the rich, both of which are anathema for it. The same reason for which Keynesian demand management is ruled out in a neo-liberal economy also rules out any welfare state measures. Even though such measures may initially be presented as mere add-ons to neo-liberalism, if they are on any significant scale, they will inevitably lead to capital flight. Succumbing to the threat posed by capital flight and hence withdrawing the welfare state measures simply means that the economy remains stuck in stagnation and the neo-fascist challenge continues. Defending the secular-democratic character of the Indian polity therefore demands a steadfast commitment to a change of course, even while ensuring that the costs of transition are minimized.

One must not underestimate the costs of transition. Even if controls on capital outflows are imposed well in time, any such control would also curb inflows and hence make a trade deficit unsustainable. Capital controls therefore have to be supplemented by trade controls, which essentially means that the development of the country will have to be based on an expansion of the home market. Land redistribution to break the hold of landlordism; support for peasant agriculture; support for petty production; reliance on the public sector; bilateral trade agreements with other countries like Iran and Russia that are also facing imperialist sanctions, for meeting our immediate energy needs; and of course the rights-based welfare state measures mentioned above: these will be the means through which the country may be able to handle a showdown with international capital, and with possible sanctions by imperialist powers that typically accompany any such showdown.

To be sure, for a broad united front of political parties to defeat neo-fascism, one cannot set such an alternative trajectory as a precondition. But one must recognize that no matter what the initial agreed programme of such a united front may be, the direction of movement will have to be towards such an alternative trajectory, if neo-fascism is to be decisively vanquished – and Sitaram was perfectly aware of this fact.

References

Baran, P.A. and Sweezy, P.M. (1966), *Monopoly Capital*, New York: Monthly Review Press.

Bilgrami, Akeel (2014), *Secularism, Identity and Enchantment*, Cambridge, Mass.: Harvard University Press.

Guerin, Daniel ([1939] 1973), *Fascism and Big Business*, New York: Pathfinder Press.

Kalecki, M. (1954), *The Theory of Economic Dynamics*, London: Allen and Unwin.

Patnaik, P. and Ghosh, J. (2020), 'For a Set of Universal Economic Rights', in Nikhil Dey, Aruna Roy and Rakshita Swamy, ed., *We the People*, New Delhi: Vintage Books.

Patnaik, U. (forthcoming), *Exploring the Poverty Question*, New Delhi: Tulika Books.

SITARAM YECHURY

Pseudo-Hinduism Exposed

What Is Hindu Rashtra?

India at 75

Pseudo-Hinduism Exposed

The Bharatiya Janata Party (BJP)–Rashtriya Swayamsevak Sangh (RSS)–Vishwa Hindu Parishad (VHP)–Bajrang Dal (BD) combine — Saffron Shirts or SS for short: the resemblance to Hitler's infamous SS and Brown Shirts is more than coincidental) — not only continues to brazenly defend the wanton destruction of the Babri Masjid, but is in fact justifying it as a great service done to the cause of the nation. In the process, it justifies its complete rejection of the Indian Constitution, law and the courts. The SS in fact today has rejected the existing political system.

The events of 6 December [1992] and later have truly demonstrated the SS's fascistic nature, not only in its aims but also in the perfidious methods and propaganda that it is adopting. Mastering the maxim of Hitler's propaganda minister Goebbels – 'If you tell a big-enough lie frequently enough, it becomes the truth' – the SS continues to perpetuate untruths in defence of its despicable actions.

A characteristic feature of a party with fascist overtones is that different leaders speak in different voices. They do so to confuse the people and mislead them by never making their true objective clear. The present-day rantings of BJP leaders and the crocodile tears they shed for destroying the secular polity seek to mask their real intention – the establishment of a Hindu Rashtra, a theocratic state which is the very antithesis of the existing democratic secular polity.

This perfidy must be unmasked. The challenge has to be squarely met to defend and uphold all that the people of our country, through generations of struggle, have achieved so far. The untruths they propagate must be thoroughly exposed.

Lie No. 1: That enraged 'Hindu sentiments' led to the pulling down of the mosque, in exasperation.

At the outset it must be emphasized that India is a secular state precisely because the predominant majority of Hindus embraced secularism, rejecting the RSS concept of Hindu Rashtra. They rejected the RSS concept as an attempt to take India back to medieval times as a religious theocratic state, which constitutes the very antithesis of a democratic polity. The majority of Hindus, through the freedom struggle, embraced values which found manifestation in our Constitution. It is precisely these values that the SS has attacked by their wanton destruction on 6 December. In the process they have not championed 'Hindu sentiments', but sought to demolish the efforts of entire generations of secular Hindus. By hiding behind the veil of 'Hindu sentiments', the SS is actually reiterating the basis of the Hindu Rashtra that was frighteningly outlined by the late RSS chief, M.S.

Golwalkar, with fascistic precision. In a book titled *We or Our Nationhood Defined*, Golwalkar bemoaned the fact that Hindus had forgotten their nationhood, and called upon them to rise to defend their nation. He wrote:

> Only those movements are truly national as aim at rebuilding, revitalizing and emancipating from its present stupor, the Hindu nation. Those only are nationalist patriots who, with the aspirations to glorify the Hindu race and nation next to their heart, are prompted into and strive to achieve that goal. All others are either traitors and enemies to the national cause, or, to take a charitable view, idiots.

And as for those who are not Hindus but have contributed to the development of their country and continue to live here, Golwalkar had this to say:

> They have no place in national life, unless they abandon their differences, adopt the religion, culture and language of the nation, and completely merge themselves in the national race. So long, however, as they maintain their racial religious and cultural differences, they cannot but be only foreigners.

Further:

> ... in Hindusthan exists, and must exist, the ancient Hindu nation, and naught else but the Hindu nation. All those not belonging to the national, i.e. Hindu race, religion, culture and language, naturally fall out of the pale of real national life.

And:

> The foreign races in Hindusthan must either adopt the Hindu culture and language, must learn to respect and hold in reverence the Hindu religion, must entertain no idea except the glorification of the Hindu religion and culture, i.e. of the Hindu nation, and must lose their separate existence to merge in the Hindu race, or they may stay in the country wholly subordinated to the Hindu nation, claiming nothing, deserving no privileges, far less any preferential treatment – not even citizen's rights. There is, at least should be, no other course for them to adopt. We are an old nation, let us deal as old nations ought to deal with the foreign races who have chosen to live in our country.

And how should one deal with such 'foreign races'? Golwalkar exposes the fascistic nature of the Saffron Brigade:

> To keep up the purity of the race and its culture, Germany shocked the world by purging the country of the semitic race – the Jews. Race pride at its highest has been manifested here. Germany has also shown how well-nigh impossible it is for races and cultures having differences going to the roots, to be assimilated into one united whole, a good lesson for us in Hindusthan to learn and profit by.

This is the meaning of the BJP's invocation of the 'Hindu sentiment'. This runs contrary to the vast diversity and majority of Hindu opinion, which has been guided more by Vivekananda and Adi Sankara than by

Golwalkar or the present-day self-incarnations of the SS put together. While Adi Sankara had constantly preached that as different rivers flow through different courses to merge in the same ocean, so do different individuals through different faiths merge with the same almighty, Vivekananda had said,

> If anybody dreams of the exclusive survival of his own religion and the destruction of others, I pity him from the bottom of my heart and point out to him that upon the banner of every religion will soon be written, in spite of resistance, help, and not fight, assimilation and not destruction, harmony and peace and not dissension.

Above all, take the *Bhagavad Gita* which says, 'Whatever celestial form a devotee seeks to worship with faith, I stabilize the faith of that particular devotee in that particular form' (chapter VII, 21). Whatever be the colour of the cow, its milk is always white. The RSS's Hindu Rashtra is in total contradiction to such wisdom. The so-called enraged 'Hindu sentiments' are nothing but a fascistic expression of pseudo-Hinduism; an expression of how religion is utilized for partisan political interests.

This runs completely in contradiction to and in conflict with the Constitution adopted by our people for Independent India: a Constitution that was drafted by a predominantly Hindu majority of the Constituent Assembly; a Constitution that continues to be defended by Hindus who are laying down their lives in struggles against the enemies of our country and uphold its unity. Which are the Hindus that the SS today seeks to champion? Can they be allowed to hijack the great traditions and ethos that constitute our social, cultural and political heritage? The SS's attempts to impose a theocratic Hindu Rashtra must be resisted tooth and nail.

***Lie No. 2*: Temples have been destroyed in the past and continue to be destroyed today. So what is wrong in destroying the Babri Masjid?**
The SS tries to justify its vandalism by pointing out the destruction of temples both in the past and the present. As far as the past is concerned, must the present generation be made to atone for those events, either substantiated or unsubstantiated? If the process of undoing historical wrongs is unleashed, then there are no limits that can be set for going back into history. The son cannot be punished for the father's crime, leave alone crimes committed by generations ago, even if these charges can be substantiated.

Deliberate untruths continue to be spread regarding the number of temples that were allegedly demolished in Kashmir. The Report of the B.G. Verghese Committee, set up and conducted at the behest of the RSS-run Deendayal Upadhyaya Research Institute and released in March 1991, showed that not a single temple in the Kashmir Valley had been destroyed recently, though some were damaged primarily as a result of being occupied by security forces.

Further, in the 1986 riots in Anantnag, the RSS rumour machine had claimed that over a hundred temples were destroyed. Both government and unofficial enquiries show that only two temples were damaged, which were rebuilt by the government within a week.

There is no dispute about it and history is witness to the desecration of many Hindu places of worship by Muslim zealots. Destruction of places of worship in medieval times was an integral part of gaining political power. However, such destruction was not confined only to Muslims. In the eleventh century, Harshadeva of Kashmir defiled a large number of temples. In the twelfth century, Subhatavarman, the Parmara ruler, plundered Jain temples in Gujarat. Any number of such examples can be given. Note that the Jagannath temple at Puri is built on the ruins of a tribal shrine. At Bodh Gaya, a Buddhist *vihara* was destroyed by Sasanka in the sixth century and in its place a Hindu temple was raised, which still exists.

All this is a part of the history through which our country has passed. And the issue was settled over the years of the freedom struggle. The Constitution of India, which is a product of the freedom struggle, in unambiguous terms gave to our people a democratic–secular polity – a polity that was necessary for the preservation of the vast multi-religious, multi-linguistic and multi-cultural character of our country. Independent India emphatically rejected the RSS concept of Hindu Rashtra. By raking up such issues of the past, the BJP today is once again placing the agenda of Hindu Rashtra before the country. As it was rejected earlier, it has to be more emphatically rejected today.

The destruction of temples is to be condemned,

so too the destruction of other places of worship. The destruction of mosques in Punjab following the Partition in 1947, the destruction of mosques in Bhagalpur in 1990, and the destruction of gurudwaras in 1984 are all, according to the SS, justifiable. Such double standards must be thoroughly exposed.

The diabolical nature of the SS can be understood by their complete lack of respect for the Hindu religion itself, when, along with the Babri Masjid, it wantonly destroyed the Ayodhya temples of Ram Chabutra and Sita ki Rasoi on 6 December. Does the SS condemn such destruction?

Finally, and importantly, by taking recourse to the destruction of temples as a justification for the destruction of the Babri Masjid, the SS is thoroughly exposing its character of operating outside the existing law and the Constitution. If temples are being desecrated in Kashmir today, it is done by anti-national secessionist forces who have rejected India's unity and Constitution. The Indian government and the state deals with them accordingly as enemies of the country. The SS, by equating itself with such anti-national secessionists, only exposes itself as a political force whose character is no different. If this is their justification for destroying the Babri Masjid, then they should also be dealt with like the anti-national secessionists are dealt with in Kashmir.

Further, the destruction of the Babri Masjid was not an isolated event confined to a communally sensitive locality. It was an event elevated to the national plane with *kar sevak*s mobilized from all over India. It symbolized the communalization of Indian politics. Hence, similar threats regarding Mathura and Varanasi, are part of anti-national activities not confined to any region or state, but covering the country as a whole.

Lie No. 3: Temples are destroyed in Islamic countries. So what is wrong in destroying the Babri Masjid?
Temples are desecrated in these countries because they are theocratic polities based on intolerance. The SS's position would not be wrong if India were a theocratic Hindu state: a state based on Hindu religious practices that not merely sanctions but glorifies criminal practices like '*sati*', that condones and encourages perpetuation of the inhuman caste inequities, and the oppression and atrocities perpetrated against 'lower' castes. This is precisely what is sought to be established, throwing us all back into medieval barbarism. This, our people rejected in the past, and continue to do so.

We condemn the attacks on temples in these countries in no uncertain manner. But the condemnation does not step there. It extends to the condemnation of a theocratic polity that ruthlessly suppresses democracy. The rabid intolerance of other religions is matched by ruthlessly suppressive laws that deny elementary democratic rights especially to women. Theocracy and democracy are incompatible, as demonstrated by the experience of many of these countries. Muslim fundamentalism that is being encouraged by some of these countries only feeds the Hindu communal forces in India. Each provides grist to the mill of the other, and together mount an attack not only on secularism but the very foundations of democracy. If India has to remain democratic, it has to remain secular as well. The SS's concept of Hindu Rashtra is not merely an assault on secularism but on democracy itself.

Lie No. 4: The Hindu majority is suffering because the Muslim minority is being pampered and appeased!
The SS buttresses its reactionary, diabolical efforts by unleashing a hate campaign against the Muslim community. The systematic spread of untruths seeks to camouflage its real ambition.

(i) *The Muslim population is growing so fast that Hindus will soon become a minority.*
The comparative figures for the 1961 and 1981 censuses (1991 data are not yet available) show that the percentage of Muslims to total population during these twenty years went up from 10.7 per cent to 11.4 per cent – an increase of a mere 0.7 per cent. The threat that the SS propagates is ridiculous, therefore.

(ii) *Muslims can have four wives while Hindus can have only one.*
Some Hindus may feel deprived on this count! But what are the facts? At the outset it must be noted that there are, today, 25 lakh Muslim women less than Muslim men!

A survey conducted by the 1961 census shows the practice of polygamy being highest amongst the tribals (15.25 per cent), while for the Hindus it was 5.8 per cent and for the Muslims it was lower still, at 5.7 per cent.

The Report of the Commission on the Status of Women (1975) revealed that during 1941 to 1951, polygamous marriages among Muslims were 0.09 per cent less than among Hindus. The figures for the period 1951 to 1961 show that Muslim polygamous marriages were 0.65 per cent less than among Hindus. The Report also showed that in the later period, the number of polygamous marriages was greater among Hindus (5.06 per cent) than Muslims (4.31 per cent).

Yet, isolated examples are circulated such as the actor Dilip Kumar having divorced his first wife to marry Saira Bano. But no mention is made of Dharmendra marrying Hema Malini while his first wife was still around.

(iii) *Muslims reject family planning and hence their population grows faster.*
An all-India survey conducted by the Operations Research Group (ORG), Baroda revealed that the number of Muslim couples practising family planning by permanent methods rose by 11.5 per cent between 1980 and 1989, while the increase was only 10 per cent for Hindus. In terms of using temporary methods the percentage of Hindus decreased by 10 per cent, while that of Muslims went up by almost 5 to 10 per cent (*Telegraph*, 14 October 1992).

(iv) *The Muslims are a pampered lot.*
Let us look at some important indicators. The average per capita income of Muslims is 5 per cent less than the national average of Rs 4,247 (*India Today*, 3 October 1992).

According to a survey conducted by the Planning Commission for 1987–88, the average literacy rate of Muslims was 42 per cent, less than the national average of 52.11 per cent. The status of women on this count was abysmal. Only 11 per cent of Muslim women were literate compared to the national average of 39.42 per cent.

A high-power committee headed by the late Dr Gopal Singh submitted a report to the Minorities Commission in 1983. This revealed that throughout the 1970s the number of Muslims who found placements in jobs and educational institutions were much less in number than the qualified and eligible sections of their population. The following chart for that decade is self-explanatory.

	Percentage of Muslims	Adequacy level (of qualified and eligible sections of the population)
Engineers	2.0	1/6
Doctors	2.5	1/5
IAS	2.86	1/4
IPS	2.0	1/6
ITOS	3.06	
State Class I	3.3	
Banks	2.18	
Private enterprises	4.08	

In the '*Garibi Hatao*' decade of the 1970s, of the total number of bank loans given for poverty alleviation programmes, Muslims received only 3.76 per cent. According to the *Economic Times* (21 December 1992), the decline in the community's relative economic strength was between 20 and 25 per cent.

This is the status of the community that supposedly poses a grave threat to the Hindus! Can such Goebbelsian untruths be allowed to divert us from our genuine struggles against the present economic policies that continue to heap ruin on millions? Can we allow the SS to take recourse to such falsehoods and subterfuge to achieve its diabolic plan to foist a reactionary, theocratic Hindu Rashtra? The enemies of modern India have to be completely and thoroughly unmasked.

(e) *Mulsims have been appeased by the Shah Bano case ruling.*

This was a blatant concession made by the Rajiv Gandhi government which goes totally contrary to the essence of a secular polity. The CPI(M) was not only in the forefront of but actively conducted a nationwide campaign, that such buttressing of Muslim fundamentalism will pose grave dangers to secularism.

In a secular polity, ideally, the civil code should be common and uniform for all citizens irrespective of their religion. But such a common civil code would mean the abandonment of not only the Muslim Personal Law, but also of various laws that are specific to the Hindu community like the Hindu Marriages Act and, more importantly, the Hindu Undivided Family Act. The latter is notoriously used to deprive the state of crores of rupees through taxes. It also means that equal rights would have to be granted to women in matters of inheritance and such other areas. The discriminatory provision against women in the Hindu Acts will also have to be abandoned. More than the Muslims, are the Hindu communalists prepared for this? All along, it has been the fundamentalists in both the communities that opposed any progressive amendments to existing laws.

It is only through the strengthening of secularism and its corresponding consciousness, and over a period of time when each and every minority community feels not only secure but has the fullest confidence that its rights are protected, that the ground for such a common civil code be created. The SS's inflammatory communal poisoning only works to the contrary. By sowing deep the seeds of discord they create conditions of growing insecurity amongst the minorities.

Lie No. 5: **Since an Islamic Pakistan has been created, why do Muslims continue to live in India? India is only meant for the Hindus.**

That India is only for the Hindus was a concept that was roundly rejected during the freedom struggle and after. The majority of the Muslims did not migrate to Pakistan and continued to live in India. There are more Muslims in India than the entire population of Pakistan. Further, India has the largest number of Muslims in the world, next only to Indonesia.

They have chosen to remain in India because Independent India adopted secularism. It is not only the Muslims but any number of religious minorities that continue to live in India since it is as much their country as anybody else's. The bulk of those who converted to other religious faiths from Hinduism were after all indigenous people. It is the interaction of these various cultures that has given India its rich diversity, which cannot be straitjacketed into any one religion. For over five centuries, the lineage of the Muslim Dagar Brothers had sung and continue to sing '*Ram dhuns*'. There are innumerable instances of exemplary patriotism by members of minority communities. It must be remembered that the first Paramvir Chakra in Independent India was given to a Muslim, Abdul Hameed.

People of other religious faiths chose to live in India because it is not a theocratic state, a Hindu Rashtra. Christians of Tamil Nadu and Kerala have been here since CE 32. The Muslims of Gujarat and Kerala have remained here since the medieval seventh century, when trading with Arabia was established. They have stayed in India longer, probably, than those who embraced Hinduism coming from Central Asia, over the seventh and eighth centuries.

The SS campaign in this context is purely inflammatory communal propaganda to further its political interests.

Lie No. 6: **That the Babri Masjid was constructed after destroying a standing Ram temple.**
There is absolutely no conclusive historical evidence to prove this. All findings of any structure prior to the Babri Masjid are equivocal and ambiguous. Some studies have

in fact suggested that Ayodhya was a revered place of Buddhism, known as Saket. And if we were to investigate, we may well find ruins of a Buddhist *stupa* there.

Prior to the present incendiary communal campaign unleashed by the SS there were half a dozen more temples in Ayodhya, whose priests used to claim that this was the actual birthplace of Lord Ram. A similar situation obtains today in Mathura.

That the SS insisted and continues to propagate that Ram was born precisely where the Babri Masjid stood was its deliberate attempt to utilize religious communal passions for its political purpose.

In fact Tulsi Das, who preserved and propagated the epic of Ramayana in his *Ram Charita Manas*, which was written soon after the construction of the Babri Masjid, makes no mention of the destruction of any temple. Surely, a Ram *bhakt* like Tulsi Das would have recorded such an outrage.

It was in fact the British who, following the 1857 revolt, consciously fostered communal divide to consolidate their rule. The dispute regarding the Babri Masjid was first propagated by British historians in order to sow seeds of discord. It must be recollected that in 1857 the heroic Rani of Jhansi, Laxmi Bai, a devout Hindu, had along with other Hindu rulers accepted the suzerainty of Bahadur Shah Zafar, the Mughal ruler of India. Amongst others who betrayed the first war of independence were the direct ancestors of a present-day SS leader, Vijaya Raje Scindia. Fostering the communal divide, the British successfully continued to enslave our country for nearly a century longer. It is now part of recorded history that communal tension as a result of such propaganda regarding the Babri Masjid was directly utilized by them to justify their annexation of Awadh.

Also, those who continue to propagate that Babar conquered the Hindus will do well to remember that Babar established the Mughal empire after defeating a Muslim ruler of Delhi, Ibrahim Lodi.

Lie No. 7: That what was destroyed on 6 December was not a mosque. Hence, why this fuss?

Advani on 8 December stated that 'The structure which ceased to be a mosque over fifty years back is pulled down.' That the Babri Masjid was physically in existence for over four-and-a-half centuries is sought to be erased. That the dispute started on 23 December 1949 when idols were surreptitiously placed is deliberately ignored. There were no idols in the mosque for over four centuries. They were placed defiling the sanctity of the mosque in the background of the communal frenzy that gripped the country following the Partition. For centuries *namaz* was read in the mosque and Hindus worshipped at Ram Chabutra, the temple that they have now destroyed. The Imam who conducted the last *namaz*, Haji Abdul Gaffar, is still alive; his son was killed in the vandalism following the destruction of the Babri Masjid on 6 December.

We are asked, why all this fuss about a decrepit structure? That this structure came to symbolize the Indian ethos because its status, based on our accepted secular Constitution, was subject to courts' jurisdiction;

that the highest court had ordered its protection till the case was disposed of; that the leaders of the Saffron Brigade assured the courts and the country of their adherence to the law; that they deliberately and wantonly destroyed the Babri Masjid in defiance of the courts, law and their own assurance – all this is of course of no concern to them. Their deceit, perfidy and total contempt for the law of the land cannot be concealed by pretending that the 'structure' was not a mosque.

Lie No. 8: **The leaders could not contain the enraged mobs!**

Notwithstanding the crocodile tears shed by the BJP leaders, it is now clear that the destruction of the Babri Masjid was the result of a pre-planned effort. It has now come to light that the entire destruction was rehearsed and meticulously pre-planned (*Statesman*, 10 December, and other newspapers). It is precisely for this reason that no mediapersons, particularly photographers, were allowed to document the destruction, and were physically assaulted and hounded out of the area.

The lie that the BJP leadership was caught unawares by the demolition is easily exposed if one carefully studies the statements made by the BJP leaders, especially Mr L.K. Advani during the week preceding 6 December. The following accounts are the ultimate in doublespeak and perfidy.

> *Varanasi, 1 December*: 'We do not want to destroy any masjid and make a mandir. There was never a masjid at

the Janmabhoomi site. The idols of Ram are there and all we want to do is build a temple there ... to democratically protest against wrong practices and law is an old tradition of the country ... karseva does not mean bhajans and kirtans. We will perform karseva with shovels and bricks on the 2.77 acres of land acquired by the U.P. Government.'

Azamgarh, 1 December: 'We want peaceful karseva but the centre is creating tension.'

Mau, 2 December: 'Now karseva will begin on 6 December. All karsevaks will perform physical activity on the 2.77 acres in Ayodhya and not merely sing bhajans.'

Gorakhpur, 3 December: Where he had described a news report quoting him as having said karseva would involve use of shovels and bricks as false: 'The karsevaks will be fully under control. The karseva will be symbolic. I never said such a thing [about shovels and bricks being used]. Yet due to this misreporting half a day's work in Parliament was lost because of the uproar this report caused.'

Public meeting in U.P., 2 December, where he exhorted people to go to Ayodhya for karseva: 'Take a plunge and do not bother whether the Kalyan Singh government survives or is dismissed.'

New Delhi, 7 December: 'It [the demolition of the mosque] was unfortunate. Both I and the U.P. chief minister did all we could to prevent the destruction but what actually happened was we could not gauge the intensity of the people's feelings over Ayodhya. We wanted that the temple should be constructed by legal and lawful means.'

New Delhi, 8 December: 'Today, when an old structure which ceased to be a mosque over 50 years back is pulled down by a group of people exasperated by the tardiness of the judicial process and the obtuseness and myopia of the executive, they are reviled by the president, the vice-president and political parties as betrayers of the nation, destroyers of the constitution and what not. It is blatant double standards such as evidenced by this tirade against the Ayodhya movement that is making the Hindus feel incensed and outraged.
(*The Statesman,* 11 December 1992)

Hence, all arguments put forward of wanting to demarcate between the hard-liners and the soft-liners within the Saffron Brigade are a deliberate exercise to mislead the people. It is the characteristic of a fascistic organisation that different leaders speak in different voices. This is precisely what the S.S. has done. Their intention all along was clear: destruction of the Babri Masjid and the establishment of a theocratic Hindu Rashtra.

Lie No. 9: That all this happened due to the intransigence of the Muslims.

We are told that Muslims should have gracefully accepted the SS's diktat and voluntarily abdicated their claims on the Babri Masjid, in which case none of this would have happened. Strange, indeed. The minority should succumb to the unreasonableness of the majority only because of the strength of the majority! In any case, this was not for the RSS an isolated issue, but the beginning of a campaign to continue their inflammatory communal propaganda for the destruction of the mosques both in Varanasi and Mathura. This was eloquently expressed by the belligerence of the BJP MPs' slogans in the Parliament on 8 and 9 December.

Lie No. 10: **That all this happened due to the procrastination of the courts.**
The fact that all assurances to the courts by the SS leaders including Kalyan Singh and Vijaye Raje Scindia were violated, and the constant refrain of 'courts cannot decide on matters of faith', have thoroughly exposed their contempt for the judiciary. The judiciary was acceptable to them as long as it upheld their view. In a democratic polity, any dispute between two faiths can be resolved either through a mutually negotiated settlement or a judicial intervention and verdict. The SS all along rejected such reason, fearing rejection of their bigotry. The now-delivered judgement of the Special Bench of the Allahabad High Court annulling the Kalyan Singh government's acquisition of the disputed land has only vindicated this. Their position always was that if the courts upheld their position, then it was acceptable – otherwise, no.

Lie No. 11**: **All this happened due to the incompetence and inept attitude of the central government!

Very true! If the government had acted in time and on the basis of the suggestions made by the CPI(M) and the Left, such a serious situation could have been averted. The government actually abdicated its political responsibility and relied on the private assurances of the leaders of the SS. For this criminal ineptitude, the CPI(M) had demanded that P.V. Narasimha Rao has no moral right to continue as the Prime Minister. The SS, however, blames the Government not for this, but for not accepting their terms! The incompetence of the present Congress (I) government, its ineptitude bordering on complicity and criminal negligence of its duties, cannot absolve the SS from the damage that has been done to our social fabric and polity.

The reality is that what we are challenged with is a force that is out to destroy the entire premise of a modern, secular, democratic India. To this effect, in pursuance of their political ambition, they have no scruples in stooping to the worst possible crimes. Thousands who continue to die in the aftermath of 6 December and thousands who have died since this inflammatory campaign was unleashed in the mid-1980s, are all sacrifices made at the altar of the fascistic pseudo-Hindu attempt to capture political power. It is this that has to be completely unmasked.

Lie No. 12**: **The BJP is the champion of democracy! The democratic rights of the SS are being curtailed today!

Even the CPI(M) has capitulated from its demand for scrapping Article 356 of the Constitution!

The SS's ultimate duplicity is the attempt to masquerade as a 'champion' of democracy. Can those who, in complete violation of the Constitution, law and courts, wantonly destroyed the Babri Masjid with meticulous pre-planning have the right to speak of, leave alone defend, democracy? Having violated all democratic foundations of the Indian Constitution, they are now crying wolf! According to them Advani and company have the right to destroy the Babri Masjid, but they cannot be arrested! BJP state governments can use official machinery to mobilize, arm and train *kar sevak*s, send them to Ayodhya to demolish the mosque, in complete violation of the Constitution under which they pledged to function. The Chief Ministers can proudly state that they are leading members of the RSS and schemingly justify the demolition. This, of course, is democratic! But if action is taken on this count, it is undemocratic! The basic norm of the existing democratic polity is that only those who function within its parameters have access to democratic rights guaranteed by the polity. The BJP by its actions has chosen to opt out of this democratic framework. By demolishing the mosque, as it chose to do, the BJP has forfeited its claim to democracy and democratic rights contained in our Constitution.

Failing to see this basic point or deliberately glossing over it, certain columnists are mounting a systematic attack in defence of the BJP by stating that the dismissal of its state governments is 'undemocratic'. In the process, the CPI(M) is being frontally attacked for an alleged capitulation from its long-standing demand for scrapping Article 356 from the Constitution.

The record needs to be set right. The CPI(M) has consistently sought the removal of Article 356, and continues to do so. This stand stems from the fact that this particular provision can be, and has been, misused to suit the political interests of the ruling party. Thus, it restricts and limits the truly federal essence of our Constitution, and to that extent it is undemocratic. The CPI(M)'s stand is thus directed at enhancing the democratic and federal content of our Constitution.

The BJP's wailing against this clause is not from this point of view. Its 'democratic' right to violate the Constitution with impunity must be accepted, but how can anyone dare to take action against its state governments! Its stand stems not from the point of enhancing the democratic content of the Constitution but from the contrary. No action can be taken against it even if it violates the very foundations of the Constitution!

Consider a hypothetical situation. Suppose, following the Punjab elections, Khalistani separatists had formed the government and adopted a resolution in the Assembly declaring secession from India. Can any central government not use the constitutional provisions to dismiss such a state government and defend our country's unity? Similarly, when state governments led by the BJP violate the Constitution in a manner as brazen as they did, can the people of the country tolerate it?

If this be so, why does the CPI(M) continue to seek the removal of Article 356? Precisely because this can be misused, as has been done repeatedly in the past. The grave challenge posed to the Constitution by the BJP governments and their consequent dismissal is probably the first time since Independence that Article 356 has been properly used. Even without Article 356 in the statute book, the unity and integrity of our country can be ensured. The Constitution provides other safeguards and provisions (like Article 355) for central government intervention in cases as serious as these. But the Congress governments have repeatedly used Article 356 because it is most convenient for its interests. The Governors, whose status has been reduced to that of mere nominees of the centre, can be utilized to give a report to suit the political interests of the ruling party at the centre.

The entire debate on the 'undemocratic' use of Article 356 in the present context, thus, only serves as a smokescreen to defend the BJP's indefensible violation of the Constitution and the utter contempt with which it holds democracy.

Democracy and secularism are inseparable in today's Indian polity. In fact, they are inseparable in any modern polity. Secularism is defined as the separation of religion from politics and the state. Unless this is ensured, no democracy exists for any minority community. By choosing to exercise democratic rights to attack secularism and instead propagate communalism of the worst order, the BJP is completely undermining the foundations of modern India. In place of a democratic–

secular republic, they seek to impose its very antithesis: the RSS concept of Hindu Rashtra.

In this context, the BJP's so-called championing of the freedom of the press must be seen in a proper light. Press freedom is championed so long as this is required for the propagation of communalism. But the moment it is utilized to oppose it, this freedom is ruthlessly attacked. The gruesome attacks on press persons on 6 December graphically illustrates this. For the SS, freedom and democracy are for the propagation of communal poison, only to be ruthlessly suppressed when these are exercised against its interests or when its purpose is served.

Meet This Challenge Squarely

Unless this challenge is unitedly combated, unless the communal frenzy is challenged with equal vigour, the very future of India for whose freedom thousands have been martyred is at stake. All patriots who have not sold their conscience to the enemies of our country, realizing these dangers, will have to forge strong unity in action against this communal monster.

To those who underestimate the dangers of the present situation we can only remind them of what a German intellectual Pastor Neimoeller had said at the time of Nazi ascendancy:

First they came for the Jews
and I did not speak out –
Because I was not a Jew.

*Then they came for the Communists
then I did not speak out –
Because I was not a Communist.
Then they came for the Catholics
and I did not speak out –
Because I was not a Catholic.
Then they came for me –
and there was no one left
to speak out for me.*

To those who consider that these developments do not affect their life and future, we can only recall the wisdom that has filtered down through the ages: 'For evil to succeed, the good has only to be silent.' Passivity in meeting this challenge can only mean peril for the individual and the country.

All patriots will have to rise to the occasion and defend India and its democratic–secular ethos.

First published as a Communist Party of India (Marxist) pamphlet in January 1993.

What Is Hindu Rashtra?

Considerable controversy has been generated, once again, around M.S. Golwalkar's book, *We or Our Nationhood Defined* (1939). The controversy centres on the embarrassment of the Saffron Brigade, which finds its real mission of establishing a Hindu Rashtra being exposed in all its fascistic glory by this book. Thus, puncturing its efforts to mislead the Indian people by posing as adherents of democracy becomes important.

Various advocates of the Saffron Brigade, in various tones, assert that it was not Golwalkar who actually wrote this book, that it was not republished after 1942, and so on. Interestingly, however, not one of them makes any substantive point by retracting any position that Golwalkar has taken.

For the benefit of those who say that this book was not written by Golwalkar but is merely a translation of the Marathi work, *Rashtra Meemansa*, by Babarao G.D. Savarkar, brother of V.D. Savarkar (as claimed by a senior official of the RSS-run Deen Dayal Upadhyaya Research Centre, New Delhi, in *Jansatta*, 7 January 1993), here is a quote from the preface written by Golwalkar on 22 March 1939, to the first edition of the book:

> In compiling this work, I have received help from numerous quarters, too many to mention. I thank them all heartily; but I cannot help separately naming one and expressing my gratefulness to him – Deshbhakta G.D. Savarkar. His work *Rashtra Meemansa* in Marathi has been one of my chief sources of inspiration and help.
>
> The manuscript of this book was ready as early as the first week of November 1938, but its appearance earlier, however desirable, was not possible due to many difficulties. (Golwalkar 1939, p. 4)

The authorship thus being beyond dispute, we can say quite certainly that the book was neither barred from re-publication nor withdrawn after 1942. (On the basis of such a claim by the same RSS official in *Jansatta*, the editor of *Navbharat Times* went to the unethical extent of appending a comment to one of my articles, that the RSS claims that it has withdrawn this book!) We have in our possession the fourth edition of the book, published in 1947 (Golwalkar 1947). Though it must be noted that in certain places offensive language has been modified (for example, 'idiots' is replaced by 'misguided'), the content remains the same. Such modification, moreover, was considered so marginal that the author does not mention it in his preface; neither is it discernible unless closely scrutinized.

An important omission from the latter edition is the foreword to the book by one 'Lok Nayak' M.S. Aney. The reasons are not far to see. Aney says:

> I also desire to add that the strong and impassioned

language used by the author towards those who do not subscribe to his theory of nationalism is also not in keeping with the dignity with which the scientific study of a complex problem like Nationalism deserves to be pursued. It pains me to make these observations in this foreword. (Golwalkar 1939, p. xviii)

Such views could not have been allowed to be propagated at a time when the RSS (Rashtriya Swayamsevak Sangh) was reaping most of the benefit of the growing communal tensions and strife preceding Partition. The inflammatory propaganda value of the book could not be undermined.

The disinformation that they are now spreading is to conceal their ideological foundations, as Golwalkar's book continues to be the clearest expression of the real nature of the Saffron Brigade's mission today. We can do no better than quote from a very sympathetic account of the RSS, J.A. Curran's *Militant Hinduism in Indian Politics: A Study of the RSS*:

> The genuine ideology of the Sangh is based upon principles formulated by its founder, Dr Hedgewar. These principles have been consolidated and amplified by the present leader in a small book called WE or OUR NATIONHOOD DEFINED, written in 1939. *'WE' can be described as the RSS 'Bible'. It is the basic primer in the indoctrination of Sangh volunteers.* Although this book was written twelve years ago, in a national context different from the contemporary one, the principles contained in it are still considered entirely applicable by the Sangh

membership. (Curran 1979, p. 39; emphasis as in the original)

The importance of this book for the RSS must be seen also in relation to Golwalkar's role in its history. Golwalkar assumed the reins as the RSS chief in 1940. Two years prior to that, in 1938, he was appointed general secretary of the RSS by Hedgewar. Incidentally, the RSS *sarsanghchalak* (chief) is always nominated by the outgoing one, and he continues in his post till death. So much for their 'democratic' credentials!

Golwalkar served in this capacity till 1973. His role, particularly in the first phase, from 1940 to 1954, has been summed up thus:

> It [Golwalkar's leadership] remains a historical source today for the RSS and its 'family', called upon to suit specific times and audiences (particularly, during riots). It is also exceptionally helpful for our understanding of precisely what the triumph of Hindutva will mean for our country. (Basu, Datta, Sarkar, Sarkar and Sen 1993, p. 25)

Golwalkar's abiding influence has been in providing the Saffron Brigade with an ideological formation, not merely in terms of ideas and principles, but also in establishing an organizational structure to achieve the aim of a fascistic Hindu Rashtra.

This was demonstrated sharply in the period following the withdrawal of the ban imposed on the RSS after the assassination of Mahatma Gandhi. (The ban was in effect from 4 February 1948 to 12 July 1949.) The RSS, eager to negotiate the withdrawal of the ban, adopted a course of deceitful compromises. Curran notes:

> *Golwalkar's announcement soon after legality had been restored, that he had given 'no agreement or assurances' to the government, was an ineffectual attempt to maintain 'face'. The provisions for elections within the organization and the promise to denounce communalism and to maintain a tolerant attitude towards other communities were quite contrary to past Sangh practice and obviously had been accepted because of government insistence.* However, these provisions have not been observed; in practice, the Sangh membership has consistently ignored them. (Curran 1979, pp. 31–32; emphasis as in the original)

Forced by the government, the RSS adopted a constitution (which till date is not available for public scrutiny). Article 3 of this document states:

> The aims and objects of the Sangh are to weld together the diverse groups within the Hindu Samaj and to revitalize and rejuvenate the same on the basis of its Dharma and Sanskriti, that it may achieve an all-sided development of the Bharatavarsha. (Quoted in Curran 1979, p. 35)

But Curran himself adds:

> The constitution gives no hint of a militant and intolerant advocacy of a Hindu state. *There is a basic difference between the formal profession of aims embodied in the constitution and actual plans of the Sangh. The Sangh*

> *abjures secrecy of ends and means, but the incompatibility of the tolerant Hindu philosophy of the constitution and the fanatically pro-Hindu and anti- non-Hindu aims instilled in the membership is clear. The proclaimed philosophy is a pale and often deceptive reflection of the real objectives of the Sangh. ...* Too open an expression of Sangh ideals would undoubtedly result in repression of RSS activities. The Sangh leaders are too shrewd to risk an open struggle with the government while the odds heavily favour the latter. (Curran 1979, pp. 35–36; emphasis as in the original)

It was in line with this that Golwalkar, in September 1949, publicly voiced in Lucknow the RSS criticism of the Indian Constitution, which he termed as 'Un-Bharat'. There is a similarity indeed here with the present leaders of the VHP (Vishwa Hindu Parishad) who describe it as 'Un-Hindu'.

Apart from such tactical manoeuvres, Golwalkar undertook certain organizational initiatives. Following the agreement with the government on the withdrawal of the ban, he went on to establish the now-infamous Sangh Parivar. The strategy was clear. The RSS would in the public eye confine itself to 'cultural activity', while its affiliates would branch out into various sections spreading the message of 'Hindu Rashtra'. These seemingly independent tentacles were welded together by the RSS. This organizational network is there today for all to see.

Golwalkar's important initiative, however, came in the attempt to organize the Hindu religious leaders in mid-1964, to discuss ways in which various Hindu sects and tendencies could sink their many differences, work together and establish contacts with Hindus residing abroad. Thus was laid the foundations of the Vishwa Hindu Parishad, and an RSS pracharak, Shivram Shankar Apte, became its first general secretary. The subsequent career of the VHP, today the most formidable of the RSS affiliates, demands a separate study. (Basu, Datta, Sarkar, Sarkar and Sen 1993, p. 50)

Another organizational measure taken by Golwalkar was to utilize this organizational structure of 'family' [*parivar*] to create a political front which would be always under the leadership and control of the RSS. In 1951, he sent cadres to help Shyama Prasad Mukherjee to start the Bharatiya Jan Sangh, whose later incarnate is today's Bharatiya Janata Party (BJP). Among those who were sent were Deen Dayal Upadhyay, Atal Behari Vajpayee, L.K. Advani and S.S. Bhandari. (This fact is mentioned in Basu, Datta, Sarkar, Sarkar and Sen 1993, p. 48.) Precisely for this reason, when Advani was arrested after the 6 December 1992 events, it was S.S. Bhandari who was the BJP's chief spokesman.

Thus, Golwalkar's role in developing the present ideological foundations of the Saffron Brigade cannot be underplayed. The entire organizational structure was to establish a political goal, and this was unambiguously articulated in the book, *We or Our Nationhood Defined*. Hence the abiding importance of this book for the Saffron Brigade. A proper understanding of the contents of this book and the intentions of the Saffron Brigade is necessary for all patriots who do not wish to see India slide into the morass of darkness and medieval theocracy.

Golwalkar begins his entire exercise by seeking to understand the word '*Swaraj*'. He begins by questioning what is '*Swa*', meaning 'We'. In the prologue to the book, he says:

> We stand for national regeneration and not for the haphazard bundle of political rights – the state. What we want is Swaraj; and we must be definite what this 'Swa' means. 'Our kingdom' – who are we? (Golwalkar 1939, p. 3)

The entire book is an elaboration of the thesis that 'we' means the Hindus, and hence *Swaraj* means Hindu Raj or Hindu Rashtra.

The basic purpose of the book was to establish that India was always a Hindu nation and continues to be one. By India here Golwalkar means the 'lands from sea to sea'. In fact, the map on the cover of the book gives an outline of his geographic limits for India, which expands from Afghanistan to Burma and includes Sri Lanka.

Golwalkar attempted to achieve this purpose through an ingenious distortion of both history and science. First, the entire diversity of culture, traditions, languages and customs of the peoples who inhabited India over centuries is sought to be straitjacketed into a monolithic 'Hinduism'. Secondly, an external enemy is created (that is, 'external' to the Hindus), hate against whom is used to whip up 'Hindu' consolidation.

Golwalkar here relied heavily on the experience of

Hitlerite fascism. Georgi Dimitrov, the indomitable anti-fascist who led the struggle of the international working class, had said:

> Fascism acts in the interests of extreme imperialists but presents itself to the masses in the guise of an ill-treated nation and appeals to outraged 'national' sentiments.

To present the RSS as such a champion, it was necessary to create a false consciousness that the Hindus have been and are deprived, and, at the same time, generate hate against the Muslims (taking the cue from Hitler's rabid anti-Semitism) to the effect that they were responsible for this. This was the precise purpose of the book.

The present-day activities and propaganda of the Saffron Brigade are based precisely on these two points that Golwalkar provided as ideological input. To achieve this, it has perfected the Goebbelsian technique of telling big-enough lies frequently enough to make them appear as the truth.

It is necessary to note at this stage that the external enemy was not identified by the RSS as the British, against whom the Indian people were then in struggle. The hate against the Muslim community was sought to be spread much deeper than that against the British by the RSS precisely because the Indian people could not be united for their 'Hindu Rashtra' against the British, since their anti-British feelings found expression in the growing strength of the united freedom movement. It was for this reason that the RSS never nailed down the British as its enemy. For that matter, it virtually boycotted, and at times opposed, the freedom struggle. Even sympathetic accounts of the RSS (*The Brotherhood in Saffron* by Walter K. Andersen and Shridhar D. Damle, 1987, amongst others) detail the virtual absence of the RSS in the freedom movement and the consequent concessions it gained from the British. Even Nanaji Deshmukh raises the question: 'Why did the RSS not take part in the liberation struggle as an organization?' (Deshmukh 1979, p. 29). The urge to establish a 'Hindu Rashtra' drove the RSS to be a virtual ally of the British. The freedom struggle and the Congress were regarded as a diversion from their objective. The animosity grew particularly after the All India Congress Committee (AICC) announced (at the Karachi Congress, 1931) that free India would be a secular, democratic republic. This was seen, and correctly, as the very antithesis of the RSS conception of a Hindu Rashtra.

Mahatma Gandhi, the tallest of devout and practising Hindus, was assassinated because he, along with the majority of the Indian people, embraced secular democracy – rejecting the RSS ideology.

Golwalkar, however, had to establish certain points in order to validate his thesis. First, it was necessary to establish that Hindus, and Hindus alone, were the original inhabitants of India. This Golwalkar did by the simple recourse to assertion. He states:

> We – Hindus – have been in undisputed and undisturbed possession of this land for over 8 or even 10 thousand

years before the land was invaded by any foreign race'; and therefore, this land 'came to be known as Hindusthan, the land of the Hindus' (Golwalkar 1939, p. 6).

There is a deliberate and total silence on the entire wealth of investigations of ancient Indian history, including the possibility of the name Hindusthan originating from people outside India who described this land as the land of the Indus river.

Having asserted this, he proceeds to 'prove' that Hindus did not come here from anywhere else. This was absolutely central to Golwalkar's political project since, if this could not be proved, then, logically, the Hindus would be as much of a 'foreign race' as anybody else who came to this land.

A remarkably perfidious exercise was employed to prove this point. All through this book Golwalkar uses the terms 'Hindu' and 'Aryan race' synonymously. He thus sets out to show that the Aryans did not migrate to India from anywhere, but originated here. All historical evidence to the contrary is dismissed as the 'shady testimony of Western scholars' (Golwalkar 1939, p. 6). The RSS guru, however, had to contend with Lokmanya Bal Gangadhar Tilak's theory of the Arctic origin of the Vedas. Golwalkar, while accepting Tilak's thesis, came up with the incredible assertion that the Arctic zone was originally that part of the world which is today called Bihar and Orissa,

> that then it moved north-east and then by a sometimes westerly, sometimes northward movement, it came to

its present position. If this be so, did we leave the Arctic Zone and come to Hindusthan or were we all along here and the Arctic Zone left us and moved away northwards in its zigzag march? We do not hesitate in affirming that had this fact been discovered during the life-time of Lok. Tilak, he would unhesitatingly have propounded the proposition that 'The Arctic Home of the Vedas' was verily in Hindusthan itself and that it was not the Hindus who migrated to that land but the Arctic Zone which emigrated and left the Hindus in Hindusthan. (Golwalkar 1939, p. 8)

Lunatic logic indeed! Granting the benefit of doubt, that Golwalkar was unaware of the advances in geological sciences and plate-tectonics (which today fairly accurately allows man to map the movement of various land masses over centuries), we ask a simple question: Even by the logic of his own argument, if the Arctic zone moved away from Bihar–Orissa, how could it leave behind the people who were inhabiting that land mass? When a land mass moves, it moves along with everything on it. People cannot be left hanging in a vacuum only to drop down when and where Golwalkar wishes! Such perfidy was employed to 'establish' that the Aryans originated in India and did not immigrate from anywhere else. This was central to the political aim of establishing a fascistic Hindu Rashtra.

In order to achieve internal consistency for such an incredible theory, Golwalkar had to resort to a gross distortion of history. Presenting the 'glory of Hindu civilization' till the time of the Mahabharata, he says that,

... we have another gap of many centuries, which the accredited history has not been able to fill. But we can surmise that the nation lived its usual life without any serious occurrence. Then came Buddha and the great Emperors of the Gupta Dynasty, Asoka, Harshavardhan, Vikramaditya, Pulakeshi, and others of whose rule of peace, power and plenty, we obtain incontrovertible evidence. The invasion of the 'world-conqueror' Alexander was a mere scratch. In fact he cannot be said to have invaded the country at all, so hasty was his retreat. (Golwalkar 1939, p. 9)

Totally ignoring – in fact rejecting – the recorded history of this period which was available to Golwalkar's generation, he straitjackets these centuries into a static time-frame whose only denominator is 'Hindu kings'. Even amongst the kings he names, why is it that the same Pulakeshin II stopped the southward march of Harshavardhana and defeated him on the banks of the Narmada river? Both were great Hindu kings, according to Golwalkar, and members of the same nationhood! His exercise defies not only history, but also the laws of social development. Why do kings fight against one another, why do empires rise and fall? Why did the slave system give way to the feudal agrarian order? Or how and why did the British succeed in subjugating 'Hindu kings' through superior arms? Why did the great Hindu nation not produce such firepower? All such questions are irrelevant to Golwalkar's exercise.

In a similar vein, revolts against oppressive Hindu

rituals and the caste order are ignored. Buddhism is described as merely a variant of Hinduism. In fact all other religions (especially Sikhism and Jainism) which originated in India are sought to be appropriated into the Hindu monolith.

Indian history for over eight hundred years is depicted as a single thread of a long war by the 'Hindu nation as a whole' against invading Muslims. However, Golwalkar says, the Hindu nation, which was finally emerging victorious, was subjugated by a new foe – the British. The First War of Independence against the British in 1857 is depicted as 'the last great nation-wide attempt to end the long war' (Golwalkar 1939, p. 11) by the Hindu nation. 'The attempt failed but even in their defeat a whole galaxy of noble Hindu patriots stands out – glorious objects of the Nation's worship' (ibid.).

Golwalkar conveniently forgets that the *symbol* of this revolt against the British, even by the heroic and devout Hindu queen, Rani Lakshmibai of Jhansi, was the Mughal monarch, Bahadur Shah Zafar! Was this a war of 'Hindus' against Muslim invaders, or of Indians for their freedom? Such facts of history, however, are irrelevant for Golwalkar. Further, he adduces five characteristics (or 'unities') which, according to him, define the nation: 'Geographical (Country), Racial (Race), Religious (Religion), Cultural (Culture) and Linguistic (Language)' (Golwalkar 1939, p. 33). The entire exercise that follows is to establish that the Hindus in India possessed all these characteristics, and hence have always been a nation.

But the task, even for Golwalkar, was not easy. Of

all, 'the knotty point is Religion and to a certain extent language' (Golwalkar 1939, p. 33). Race, for him, is 'by far the most important ingredient of a Nation' (ibid., p. 21). It is for this reason that he always used the terms Hindu and Aryan synonymously. Historical evidence, of course, is irrelevant.

According to the entire body of his argument, the Indus Valley civilization would be an indigenous Aryan civilization. In which case, why did it disintegrate? What were the internal causes? If this civilization was over-run from outside, who were these people? After coming into this land, did these people continue to live here or did they go back? And if evidence points to the fact that they continued to live here, what was the race that emerged as a result of this admixture? All these questions were as inconvenient for Golwalkar as historical evidence is inconvenient for the Saffron Brigade today. Such questions are countered by the formidable assertion of 'matters of faith'. Noted historian Romila Thapar, for example, says,

> The linguistic evidence of Vedic Sanskrit supports the coming into India of an Indo-European language from Iran but does not support the notion that India was the homeland of the Aryan-speaking people. (See *Seminar*, 400, December 1992; also *Seminar*, 364, December 1989)

Golwalkar dismisses all such historical evidence in a footnote:

> But obsessed with the idea that Aryans came to

Hindusthan from somewhere near the Caspian Sea or the Arctic region or some such place, and invaded this land in bands of marauders, that later they settled down first in the Punjab and gradually spread eastward along the Gunga, forming kingdoms at various places, at Ayodhya among them, the Historian feels it an anachronism, that the kingdom of Ayodhya in the Ramayan should be older than the more western Pandava Empire at Hastinapur. And he, with pedantic ignorance, teaches us that the story of the Mahabharat is the older. Unfortunately such misconceptions are stuffed into the brains of our young ones through textbooks appointed by various universities in the country. It is high time that we studied, understood and wrote our history ourselves, and discarded such designed or undesigned distortions. (Golwalkar 1939, pp. 5–6)

The inspiration for the BJP state governments to change syllabi and curricula in accordance with such an understanding originates in this source. However untenable this theory may be, it was on this basis that Golwalkar asserted the overall supremacy of religion in social life. This had little to do with religiosity. This had to be established to achieve the political objective he set out for the RSS. He dismissed the modern concept of secularism where religion is separated from both politics and the state, and treated as an individual question. Treating secularism as virtual blasphemy, he argued:

> There is a general tendency to affirm that Religion is an individual question and should have no place in

> public and political life. This tendency is based upon a misconception of Religion, and has its origin in those, who have, as a people, no religion worth the name. (Golwalkar 1939, p. 23)

Since no other religion is worth its name except Hinduism, he asserted:

> Such Religion – and nothing else deserves that name – cannot be ignored in individual or public life. It must have a place in proportion to its vast importance in politics as well. … Indeed politics itself becomes, in the case of such a Religion, a small factor to be considered and followed solely as one of the commands of Religion and in accord with such commands. (Golwalkar 1939, p. 24)

He thus negated the historical experience – of different nations having the same state religion or secular nations having no state religion, and the existence of multinational states – and the scientific validity of the fact that religion has nowhere and at no time cemented national unity. The fact that Islamic Bangladesh separated from Muslim Pakistan as a result of the national struggle of the Bangladeshi people despite a common religion is, of course, uncomfortable for such a standpoint to consider. But it was necessary for Golwalkar to assert the overall supremacy of religion for his political project.

Golwalkar's ingenious perfidy is, however, in relation to language. The multitude of languages that exist in our country, each with its own history, culture and tradition, and the fact that nationalities have emerged on this basis and continue to coexist, is dismissed with contempt.

> It appears as if the linguistic unity is wanting, and there are not one but many 'Nations', separated from each other by linguistic differences. But in fact that is not so. There is but one language, Sanskrit, of which these many 'languages' are mere offshoots, the children of the mother language. Sanskrit, the dialect of the Gods, is common to all from the Himalayas to the ocean in the South, from East to West, and all the modern sister languages are through it so much inter-related as to be practically one. It needs but little labour to acquire a going acquaintance with any tongue. And even among the modern languages Hindi is the most commonly understood and used as a medium of expression between persons of different provinces. (Golwalkar 1939, p. 43)

Such incredible logic, however, is only applicable to India. Many a European nation uses a common language, or their languages have been the off-shoots of a single Indo-European mother. They exist, because of different languages and accompanying cultures and traditions, as different nations and nationalities today. This is however irrelevant for Golwalkar, as the purpose of his exercise, divorced from scientific analysis and historical experience, was to straitjacket Indian diversity into a monolithic unity for political ends.

It is precisely on the basis of this understanding that the Saffron Brigade all along opposed, and continues to oppose, the linguistic reorganization of states. It is of course of no concern to them that at least Tamil and

Kashmiri have their origin in a non-Sanskrit group of languages. Or that Sanskrit itself was a branch of Indo-European languages which evolved and developed in this part of the world. The Saffron Brigade's opposition to Urdu, a language that fully and thoroughly evolved only in India, and its efforts to impose Hindi, are also to be traced to this source. Its current slogan, 'Hind, Hindi, Hindusthan', portends what its political project holds for the future of crores of non-Hindi-speaking people.

Golwalkar finds himself in complete isolation from both the western concept of a nation and that of the concept found in the Indian scriptures. He himself said: 'For the Rashtra concept to be complete it should be composed of "Desh" country, "Jati" race or "Janpad" people' (Golwalkar 1939, p. 52). But in order to reconcile his theory, he conveniently twisted this understanding to assert that though 'no mention is found of the three components Religion, Culture and Language' [in the ancient Indian scriptures], 'the concept of "Janpad" explicitly includes these' (ibid.).

Having thus 'established' that the Hindus were always, and continue to remain, a nation on the basis of an unscientific and ahistorical analysis, Golwalkar proceeds to assert the intolerant, theocratic content of such a Hindu nation.

> The conclusion is unquestionably forced upon us that ... in Hindusthan exists and must needs exist the ancient Hindu nation and naught else but the Hindu Nation. All those not belonging to the national, i.e., Hindu Race,

> Religion, Culture and Language, naturally fall out of the pale of real 'National' life.
>
> We repeat: in Hindusthan, the land of the Hindus, lives and should live the Hindu Nation – satisfying all the five essential requirements of the scientific nation concept of the modern world. Consequently only those movements are truly 'National' as aim at rebuilding, revitalizing and emancipating from its present stupor, the Hindu Nation. Those only are nationalist patriots, who, with the aspiration to glorify the Hindu race and nation next to their heart, are prompted into activity and strive to achieve that goal. All others are either traitors and enemies to the National cause, or, to take a charitable view, idiots. (Golwalkar 1939, pp. 43–44).

He continues:

> We must bear in mind that so far as 'nation' is concerned, all those who fall outside the five-fold limits of that idea can have no place in the national life, unless they abandon their differences, adopt the religion, culture and language of the Nation and completely merge themselves in the National Race. So long, however, as they maintain their racial, religious and cultural differences, they cannot but be only foreigners. (Golwalkar 1939, p. 45)

And further:

> There are only two courses open to the foreign elements, either to merge themselves in the national race and adopt its culture, or to live at its mercy so long as the national race may allow them to do so and to quit the

> country at the sweet will of the national race. ... From this standpoint, sanctioned by the experience of shrewd old nations, the foreign races in Hindusthan must either adopt the Hindu culture and language, must learn to respect and hold in reverence Hindu religion, must entertain no idea but those of the glorification of the Hindu race and culture, i.e., of the Hindu nation and must lose their separate existence to merge in the Hindu race, or may stay in the country, wholly subordinated to the Hindu Nation, claiming nothing, deserving no privileges, far less any preferential treatment – not even citizen's rights. There is, at least should be, no other course for them to adopt. We are an old nation; let us deal, as old nations ought to and do deal, with the foreign races, who have chosen to live in our country. (Golwalkar 1939, pp. 47–48)

And how should such 'old nations' deal with 'foreign races'? The adulation of fascist Germany could not have been more naked.

> The ancient Race spirit, which prompted the Germanic tribes to over-run the whole of Europe, has re-risen in modern Germany, with the result that the Nation perforce follows aspirations, predetermined by the traditions left by its depredatory ancestors. Even so with us: our Race spirit has once again roused itself as is evidenced by the race of spiritual giants we have produced, and who today stalk the world in serene majesty. (Golwalkar 1939, p. 32)

Further:

> To keep up the purity of the Race and its culture, Germany

shocked the world by her purging the country of the Semitic Races – the Jews. Race pride at its highest has been manifested here. Germany has also shown how well nigh impossible it is for Races and cultures, having differences going to the root, to be assimilated into one united whole, a good lesson for us in Hindusthan to learn and profit by. (Golwalkar 1939, p. 35)

Hitler thus emerges as the 'Guruji's guru'. This in fact exposes the diabolic nature of the RSS's political project. It has no compunction in borrowing a thoroughly modern and western concept of fascism, but making it appear in the garb of upholding the Hindu religion and all that is ancient. All other western concepts and civilizational advances are condemned as 'alien', except for fascism!

There is a glaring inconsistency, however, which does not seem to bother Golwalkar. If, according to him, the Hindus were Aryans, who then were these Aryans that Hitler was championing? If those were also Aryans, then did they migrate from India to Germany or vice versa? According to Golwalkar's theory, both India and Germany should be part of a single nation!

The whole exercise, thus, provides the ideological basis for a fascistic Hindu Rashtra, which continues to be the kernel of the present-day Saffron Brigade's mission.

Two other important aspects of the book must be discussed. The first relates to the question of minorities. Castigating the minority treaties laid down by the League of Nations, Golwalkar says:

> Our modern solution of the minorities problem is far more dangerous. It confers untold rights not only on those who by their number and years of residence (we doubt it) may be considered according to the League as minorities, but also on all else, howsoever few or recent in their settlement – rights and privileges far in excess of the minimum advocated by the League. The natural consequences are even now felt and Hindu National life runs the risk of being shattered. *Let us take heed and be prepared.* (Golwalkar 1939, pp. 49–50; emphasis added)

Seen together with the earlier-noted intolerance of the minorities, this understanding maps out a vision of purges that may well put to shame Nazi fascism – if the Saffron Brigade succeeds in establishing its concept of a Hindu Rashtra.

The second aspect refers to its conception of the social order in its Hindu Rashtra. Golwalkar acclaims Manu as the 'first and greatest law giver of the world', who

> lay down in his code, directing all the peoples of the world to go to Hindusthan to learn their duties at the holy feet of "eldest born" Brahmins of this land' (Golwalkar 1939, pp. 55–56).

Now, what does the *Manusmriti* say?

> [Consumption of] liquor, slaying women, Shudras, Vaishyas, or Kshatriyas [i.e. all except Brahmin men] are all minor offences. (*Manusmriti*, XI: 67)

> A Brahmin may take possession of the goods of a Shudra with perfect peace of mind, for, since nothing at all should belong to the Shudra as his own, he is one whose property can be taken away by his master. (*Manusmriti*, VIII: 417)
>
> As woman cannot utter the Vedic mantras, she is as untruth is. (*Manusmriti*, IX: 18)
>
> Indeed, an accumulation of wealth should not be made by a Shudra even if he is able to do so, for the sight of mere possession of wealth by a Shudra injures the Brahmins. (*Manusmriti*, X: 129)
>
> The wealth of the Shudra shall be dogs and donkeys. The dress of the Shudra shall be the garments of the dead, their food they shall eat from broken dishes, black iron shall be their ornaments and they must always wander from place to place. (*Manusmriti*, X: 52)

It is not as though such love for the *Manusmriti* was confined only to this book by Golwalkar. Much later, in his *Bunch of Thoughts*, he said:

> Brahmin is the head, King the hands, Vaishya the thighs and Shudra the feet. This means that the people who have thus, four-fold arrangement, i.e. the Hindu people, is our God. (Golwalkar 1966, p. 25)

It is this understanding that prompted the RSS to oppose the amendments to the 'Hindu Code Bill' after Independence, and it is this understanding that today propels the Saffron Brigade affiliates to reassert the *Manusmriti*. Witness the aggression at the recently held '*Dharam Sansad*' and the castigating of the present Indian Constitution as 'non-Hindu'.

In this context, the significance of upper-caste Maharashtra Brahmins being the leaders of the RSS till date must be noted.

> The centrality of Maharashtra in the formation of the ideology and organization of Hindutva in the mid-1920s might appear rather surprising, as Muslims here were a small minority and hardly a threat, and there had been no major riots in this region during the early 1920s. But Maharashtra had witnessed a powerful anti-Brahmin movement of backward castes from the 1870s onwards, when Jyotiba Phule had founded his Satyashodhak Samaj. By the 1920s, the Dalits, too, had started organizing themselves under Ambedkar. Hindutva in 1925 as in 1990–91, was an upper-caste bid to restore a slipping hegemony. (Basu, Dutta, Sarkar, Sarkar and Sen 1993, pp. 10–11)

The vision of a social order under the Hindu Rashtra is thus one which legitimizes both the inhuman caste oppression and the denial of elementary rights to women. Under such a dispensation, criminal practices such as *sati* may not only be legitimized, but may well be glorified.

This vision outlined by Golwalkar continues to form the basis for the Saffron Brigade to establish its vision of a Hindu Rashtra. If it today claims not to have re-published this book in the 1950s, it has little to do with repudiating this vision. If this was so at all, then it was due more to the defeat of fascism in the Second World War and the liberation of millions from its oppressive yoke. With the Golwalkar-formulated ideal having been smashed, the Saffron Brigade could not propagate it in India. Domestically, following the assassination of Gandhiji, its offensive remarks about the Congress could not have been much of a comfort.

But the essential understanding outlined in the book, as noted earlier, continues to be the inspiration for the Saffron Brigade today. The dual objective is: attempt to straitjacket the internal diversity amongst the 'Hindus' under a single domination, and generate hate against a community outside of the Hindus – the Muslims. (For an exposure of the falsehood on the basis of which the Saffron Brigade spreads this hatred, see *Pseudo-Hinduism Exposed: The Saffron Brigade's Myths and Reality*, January 1993.) [Included in this book, pp. 33–61.]

As a digression, it would be interesting to note that even the symbols around which they seek internal unification of the Hindu people – Ram and Ramayana – have very rich diversity. I recollect from my childhood the untenable characters in the Ramayana, the kings south of the Vindhyas like Vali, Sugreeva and Jambavanta, who are depicted as animals and not humans. Was this not a reflection of the attempt of Aryan domination over the Dravidians?

Or, take the legend around the festival of Onam celebrated in Kerala. The people of Kerala celebrate the annual return of their favourite king Mahabali, who is described in the Aryan version as the king of the *asuras* (demons) who had to be killed by Vishnu in the form of Vamanavatara.

A hero for one set of Hindus is a villain for another! (The Saffron Brigade, however, may say that these kings were different. Like the 'sants' who, when man landed on the moon, screamed that this moon was different from the one referred to in the scriptures.)

Or, for that matter, take the entire interpretation of *Ravanayana*, which describes the epic as the story of Ravana, who, having earned the ultimate boon of not being killed by any living creature, gets fed up with mortal life and engineers that God comes down in the form of Rama, to be killed by his hands to achieve *moksha*. *Vijaya Dashami* day, instead of marking the triumph of good over evil, could well mark the *moksha* of Ravana! (Refer Paula Richman 1992.)

In fact, the *Kamba Ramayana* in Tamil is found as a version authored by one Kampan in Thailand, adorning the galleries of the royal palace in Bangkok. A rich story of epic proportions which, as Kampan says, 'spreads, ceaselessly various, one and many at once', is today being straitjacketed for the political purposes of establishing a fascistic Hindu Rashtra.

To return to Golwalkar: in the epilogue to his book he says,

> All past civilizations 'had their day, abode a day or two and passed away,' because they had nothing to fulfil. We, however, live on, despite far greater calamities, and ever emerge triumphant masters of the world. We have

no reason to lose hope. 'Act first ... a stage so gloamed with woe, We all but sicken at the shifting scenes. And yet be patient, our Play Wright "will" show, in some fifth Act what this wild drama means. Let us be patient.' [*sic*] (Golwalkar 1939, p. 65)

The 'wild drama' is unfolding its fascistic proportions. Georgi Dimitrov (in his Address to the Seventh Congress of the Communist International, 1935) said that fascism,

> while acting in the interests of the most reactionary circles of imperialism, intercepts the disappointed masses who deserted the old bourgeois government with its irreconcilable attitude to the old bourgeois parties.

Note today the vehemence with which the Saffron Brigade mounts its attack on the very fundamental pillars of secularism and democracy that define the polity of independent India. Note also the vehemence with which it today places the entire blame for the wanton destruction of the Babri Masjid at the doorstep of the present government policies, and not as an act committed by the Saffron Brigade in flagrant violation of the existing Constitution and the law of the land.

Further, Dimitrov said:

> Fascism puts the people at the mercy of the most corrupt and venal elements but comes before them with the demand for an honest and incorruptible government speculating on the profound disillusionment of the masses ... fascism adapts its demagogy to the peculiarities of

each country, and the mass of petty bourgeois and even a section of the workers, reduced to despair by want, unemployment and insecurity of their existence, fall victim to the social and chauvinist demagogy of fascism.

It is precisely this feature of fascism that defines the demagogy and campaigns of the Saffron Brigade today. Utilizing the discontent arising out of the bourgeois–landlord class policies, they are attempting to divert this, not into channels that will reverse the conditions of impoverishment which continue to grow, but into religious communal channels, to advance their objectives. By placing before the people the construction of the Ram Janmabhoomi temple as the only agenda, the Saffron Brigade, in fact, is strengthening the very edifice of exploitation that is heaping miseries on our people. In conjunction with the open attempt to seek imperialist patronage for its purpose, this spells doom for the Indian people.

The Saffron Brigade today has clearly revealed that the actual conditions of the people and the alleviation of their miseries are not its concern. That more Indians than the entire population of the United States live below an abysmally low poverty line, is of no concern to it. That children in our country, outstripping in millions the entire population of many a country, are forced to earn a livelihood, is of no concern to it. That more Indians die every year from malnutrition than the entire population of Australia, is of no concern to it. Can such a diversion of the people's discontent for political ambitions be allowed? In the name of Ram, the Saffron Brigade today seeks to consign crores of Indians to conditions of growing impoverishment. Golwalkar and the Saffron Brigade would, however, say, 'it is not these that are our bane, but the dormancy of National feeling' (Golwalkar 1939, p. 62).

The agenda that the Saffron Brigade poses before the country and the methods that it uses to achieve its objective are nothing but an expression of an Indian variant of fascistic rule. Both in terms of the form of the state and in terms of its economic and social policies, the BJP has exposed itself as the most reactionary section of the ruling classes. The present attempt by the Saffron Brigade is not merely one of establishing a medieval theocratic 'Hindu Rashtra', but one of negating the very basis of democracy. The Saffron Brigade's agenda has to be defeated in order to safeguard modern India. Unless India is saved, it cannot be changed for the better.

Two years after Golwalkar's book was published, the Jamaat-e-Islami was founded, on 26 August 1941, under the leadership of Maulana Abul Ala Maududi, with the founding conference being held in Pathankot. Maududi is to the Jamaat what Golwalkar is to the RSS. The similarity of their political project and roles is indeed remarkable. Just as Hitler was a hero for Golwalkar, so was he for Maududi. Just as Golwalkar rejected everything modern in human civilization – liberty, equality, fraternity, secularism, democracy and parliamentary institutions – as 'alien concepts', so did Maududi and the philosophy of Muslim fundamentalism.

Maududi, in a speech at Pathankot in May 1947, when Partition was imminent, urged Indians to organize their state and society on the basis of Hindu scriptures and laws, just as they would organize Pakistan based on the laws laid down by 'Allah'. He said:

> If a Hindu government based on Hindu law came to India and the law of Manu became the law of the land as a result of which Muslims were treated as untouchables and were not given any share in the government, they did not even get the citizenship rights, I would have no objection. (Quoted in Nizami 1975, p. 11)

Hindu communalism and Muslim fundamentalism feed on each other. In the process, both spread communal poison deeper, threatening our country's unity and integrity. Both act against the interests of the majority of the people they claim to represent. India today is a secular democracy because a majority of the Hindus and Muslims rejected this politics. It is this axis of Hitler–Golwalkar–Maududi that has to be politically defeated to preserve India today. All patriots who have not sold their conscience to the enemies of the nation have to rise as one to meet this fascistic challenge.

References

Andersen, W. and Damle, Sridhar D., *The Brotherhood in Saffron: The Rashtriya Swayamsevak Sangh and Hindu Revivalism*, New Delhi: Vistaar Publications, 1987.

Basu, Tapan, Datta, Pradip, Sarkar, Sarkar, Sarkar, Tanika and Sen, Sambuddha, *Khaki Shorts: Saffron Flags*, Tracts for the Times 1, New Delhi: Orient Longman, 1993.

Curran, J.A., *Militant Hinduism in Indian Politics: A Study of the RSS*, The All India Quami Ekta Sammelan, 1979.

Deshmukh, Nana, *R.S.S.: Victim of Slander*, New Delhi: Vision Books, 1979.

Golwalkar, M.S., *We or Our Nationhood Defined*, with a foreword by Loknayak M.S. Aney, Bharat Publications: 1, 1939, Re. 1.

Golwalkar, M.S., *We or Our Nationhood Defined*, Bharat Prakashan: 1, fourth edition, 1947, Re. 1.

Golwalkar, M.S., *Bunch of Thoughts*, Bangalore: Vikrama Prakashan, 1966.

Nizami, Z.A., *Jamaat-e-Islami: Spearhead of Separatism*, New Delhi: Ministry of Information and Broadcasting, Government of India, 1975.

Richman, Paula, ed., *Many Ramayanas: The Diversity of a Narrative Tradition in South Asia*, New Delhi: Oxford University Press, 1992.

Thapar, Romila, 'The Perennial Ayrans', *Seminar*, no. 400, December 1992.

Yechury, Sitaram, *Pseudo-Hinduism Exposed: The Saffron Brigade's Myths and Reality*, a CPI(M) Publication, New Delhi, 1993.

First published in Frontline, *12 March 1993.*

India at 75

As we approach the 75th anniversary of India's Independence, a new narrative is being scripted to metamorphose our secular–democratic, Constitutional Republic into a fascistic '*Hindutva Rashtra*'. This new narrative is the complete negation of and the antithesis of India's epic struggle for freedom and the Indian state that was established under the Indian Constitution.

This new narrative suggests that while we achieved our Independence on 15 August 1947, India's real freedom was achieved with the abrogation of Article 370 and 35A of our Constitution, the dissolution of the state of Jammu and Kashmir on 5 August 2019, and the formal launching of the Ram temple construction in Ayodhya on 5 August 2020.

This narrative is based on many distortions of history, and assertions that are ahistorical and unscientific. These relate to the very conception of India as a country, nationalism, the RSS's role in the freedom struggle, etc., among many others. These need to be evaluated properly to meet and defeat this challenge.

A Battle of Visions

This new narrative did not emerge overnight. It is the product of a nearly century-long struggle between contending political, ideological visions during the freedom movement. It is therefore necessary to re-evaluate many concepts that emerged in this churning.

The withdrawal of the Non-Cooperation movement launched in 1921 by Mahatma Gandhi after the 'Chauri Chaura incident', the founding of the Communist Party of India in 1921 and the founding of the RSS in 1925 heralded an intense battle of visions on what ought to be, in the future, the character of a free India and its state structure.

A continuous battle between three visions emerged on what must be the political, social, economic and cultural character of the independent state of India. Recognizing the Indian reality of rich plurality and diversity, both the Congress and the Communists concluded that the unity of India as a country and of its people can be consolidated only when the threads of commonality in this rich diversity are strengthened, and every aspect of this plurality – linguistic, ethnic, religious, cultural – is respected and treated on the basis of equality. This recognized the fact that any effort to impose uniformity on this diversity will only lead to a social implosion.

On the basis of this understanding, the mainstream Congress vision had articulated that independent India should be a secular–democratic Republic. The Communist vision, while concurring with this objective, went further to envision that in order to consolidate the secular–democratic Republic, the political freedom of the country must be extended to achieve the socio-economic freedom of every individual, possible only under socialism.

Antagonistic to both these was the third vision, which argued that the character of independent India should be determined by the religious affiliations of its people. This vision had a twin expression – the Muslim League championing an 'Islamic State' and the Rashtriya Swayamsevak Sangh (RSS) championing a 'Hindu Rashtra'. The former succeeded with the unfortunate Partition of the country – admirably engineered, aided and abetted by the British colonial rulers – with all its consequences that continue to fester tensions and prejudices to date. The latter, having failed to achieve their objective at the time of Independence, continued with their efforts to transform modern India into their project of a rabidly intolerant, fascistic 'Hindu Rashtra'.

In a sense, the ideological battles and the political conflicts in contemporary India are a continuation of the battle between these three visions. Needless to add, the contours of this battle will continue to define the direction and content of the process of realization of the 'Idea of India'. (We shall return to this concept subsequently.)

Capitalist Path of Development

The Communists maintained that the mainstream Congress vision of consolidating the secular–democratic foundations of our Republic can succeed only when independent India frees itself from its bondage to imperialism, on the one hand, and breaks the stranglehold of feudal vestiges, on the other. The Congress party's inability to take the freedom struggle to this logical culmination became clear by its serving the interests of the post-independent ruling classes – the bourgeoisie in alliance with the landlords, led by the big bourgeoisie – pursuing the path of capitalist development. This, by itself, weakens the foundations of a secular–democratic Republic.

How? First, it relegates the anti-imperialist social consciousness that forged the unity of the people during the freedom struggle to the background, thus permitting and buttressing a social consciousness dominated by caste and communal passions. Secondly, instead of strengthening an *inclusive* India, it progressively *excludes* the growing majority of the exploited people. This was resoundingly vindicated by our experience during the first six decades of Independence. This provided the grist to the mill of the communal forces, or the third vision, to strengthen itself, exploiting growing popular discontent against the policies pursued by the ruling classes.

Thus, a mere declaration of safeguarding the secular–democratic Republic and its reassertion today remains limited in its ability to safeguard and strengthen secular–democratic India.

Perpetuating Pre-Capitalist Social Consciousness
There is another equally important factor that prevents the realization of the 'Idea of India'. The path of capitalist

development being pursued by the ruling classes is one where there is increasing collaboration with international finance capital and compromise with feudal landlords. The Indian capitalist path of development, hence, is not along the classic lines of capitalism rising from the ruins of feudalism, but in compromise with it.

The inability to eliminate the vestiges of feudalism means, at the level of the superstructure, the perpetuation of a social consciousness associated with feudalism and other pre-capitalist formations. The domination of religion and caste, integral to the social consciousness of pre-capitalist formations, continues to remain powerful in today's social order. The efforts at superimposing capitalism over feudal vestiges only creates a situation where the backwardness of consciousness associated with feudal vestiges is combined with the degenerative hedonistic 'consumerism' of today's globalized capitalist consciousness.

The process of class formation in India as a consequence of such circumscribed capitalist development is thus taking place within the parameters of the historically inherited structures of a caste-divided society. It is taking place not by overthrowing the pre-capitalist social relations, but in compromise with it. This results in an overlapping commonality between the exploited classes and oppressed castes in contemporary India. Class struggles in India, therefore, can advance only through simultaneous struggles against both – economic exploitation and social oppression.

Thus, at the level of the superstructure, feudal

decadence is combined with capitalist degeneration to produce a situation where growing criminalization of the society coexists and grows in the company of such social consciousness dominated by caste and communal feelings. Instead of overcoming such consciousness for the realization of the 'Idea of India', precisely these elements are promoted by the Hindutva forces for their political-electoral benefits.

Such a reality provides the fertile ground that engenders the current rightward shift in Indian politics buttressing the efforts for the negation of the 'Idea of India' and the establishment of a fascistic 'Hindu Rashtra' in its place.

The 'Idea of India': Nationalism

The emergence of nation-states with its attendant nationalism was integral to the long process of transition of human civilization from the stage of feudalism and capitalism. This period also threw up in Europe, the struggle for the separation of the State from the Church. The triumph of capitalism over feudalism, at the same time, signified the separation of the political authority from the myth of a divine sanction to rule invoked by kings and emperors across civilizations during the high-time of feudalism. The agreements of Westphalia finally signed in 1648 laid down the principles of sovereignty of the nation-state and the consequent international laws, which are widely believed to have established an international system on the basis of the principle of the sovereignty of states; the principle of equality between states; and the principle of non-intervention by one state in the internal affairs of another state – usually referred to as the Westphalian system. Westphalian peace was negotiated between 1644 and 1648 by the major European powers.

During the course of the defeat of fascism in World War II and the consequent dynamics of decolonization, peoples' struggles for freedom from colonialism threw up many constructs of Nationalism and the character of the State in independent countries. Such constructs arose out of long struggles in individual countries against colonialism, including in India, during this period.

The 'Idea of India': Indian Nationhood

The concept of the 'Idea of India' emerged during the epic people's struggle for India's freedom from British colonialism. *What is this 'Idea of India'?* To put it in simple terms though conscious of its multiple, complex dimensions, this concept represents the idea that India as a country moves towards transcending its immense diversities in favour of a substantially inclusive unity of its people.

Professor Akeel Bilgrami, in his introduction to an issue of the journal *Social Scientist*, containing revised versions of lectures on the relations between politics and political economy in India, given at a seminar in 2010 at the Heyman Center for the Humanities at Columbia University, New York (which he chaired then), says the following about my observations on the 'Idea of India':

[This] might be viewed as an ideal of a nation that rejects the entire trajectory in Europe that emerged after the Westphalian peace. What emerged then (and there) was a compulsion to seek legitimacy for a new kind of state, one that could no longer appeal to older notions of the 'divine right' of states personified in their monarchs. It sought this legitimacy in a new form of the political psychology of a new kind of subject, the 'citizen', a psychology based on a *feeling* for a new form of entity that had emerged, the 'nation'. This feeling, which came to be called 'nationalism', had to be generated in the populace of citizens, and the standard process that was adopted in Europe for generating it was to find an *external* enemy *within*, the outsider, the 'other' in one's midst (the Irish, the Jews, to name just two), to be despised and subjugated. At a somewhat later time, with the addition of a more numerical and statistical form of discourse, these came to be called 'minorities', and the method by which this feeling for the nation was created came to be called 'majoritarianism'. (Bilgrami 2011)

The RSS–BJP (Bharatiya Janata Party) objective of replacing the secular–democratic modern Indian Republic with their concept of a 'Hindu Rashtra' is, in a sense, a *throwback* to the Westphalian model where the Hindu majority subjugates other religious minorities (mainly Muslim: the *external* enemy *within*) to foster 'Hindu nationalism' as against 'Indian nationhood'. This, in fact, represents a *throwback* to notions of nationalism that dominated the intellectual discourse prior to the sweep of the Indian people's struggle for freedom. Such a state, based on 'majoritarianism' – their version of a rabidly intolerant, fascistic 'Hindu Rashtra' – negates the core around which emerged the consciousness of Indian nationhood contained in the 'Idea of India', as a reflection of the emergence of 'a political psychology of a new kind'.

The RSS–BJP ideologues dismiss the 'Idea of India' as a mere idea – a metaphysical concept. They reassert as a given reality, Indian (Hindu) nationalism. The RSS–BJP today are spearheading the most reactionary 'throwback' to Indian (Hindu) nationalism as against the Indian nationhood (the 'Idea of India') consciousness that emerged from the epic people's struggle for freedom from the British colonial rule. Akeel Bilgrami asserts this:

> The prodigious and sustained mobilization of its masses that India witnessed over the last three crucial decades of the freedom struggle could not have been possible without an alternative and *inclusionary* ideal of this kind to inspire it. (Bilgrami 2011)

India's diversity – linguistic, religious, ethnic, cultural – is incomparably vaster than in any other country the world knows of. Officially it has been recorded, on an earlier occasion, that there are at least 1,618 languages in India, 6,400 castes, 6 major religions of which 4 originated in these lands, 6 anthropologically defined ethnic groups – all these put together being politically administered as one country. A measure of this diversity is that India celebrates 29 major religious–cultural festivals, and probably has the largest number of religious holidays amongst all countries of the world.

Those who argue that it was the British that united this vast diversity ignore the fact that it was the British which engineered the partition of the subcontinent, leading to over a million deaths and communal transmigration of a colossal order. British colonialism has the ignominious history of leaving behind legacies that continue to fester wounds through the partition of countries they had colonized – notably, Palestine and Cyprus, apart from the Indian subcontinent. It is the pan-Indian people's struggle for freedom that united this diversity and integrated more than 660 feudal princely states into modern India, giving shape to a pan-Indian consciousness.

The Role of the Communists

The Indian Communists played an important role in this process of the evolution of the 'Idea of India'. Indeed, for this very reason, given the Communists' visionary commitment to the long struggle for freedom, the Communists' role is absolutely central to the realization of the 'Idea of India' in today's conditions.

Consider this with reference to three issues that continue to constitute, today, the core of the 'Idea of India'.

The Land Question

The struggles on the land question unleashed by the Communists in various parts of the country in the 1940s particularly – Punnapra Vayalar in Kerala, the Tebhagha movement in Bengal, the Surma Valley struggle in Assam, the Warli uprising in Maharashtra, etc., the highlight being the armed struggle in Telangana – brought the issue of land reforms to centre stage. The consequent abolition of the zamindari system and landed estates drew the vast mass of India's peasantry into the project of building the 'Idea of India'. These struggles contributed the most to liberating crores of people from feudal bondage. This also contributed substantially to creating today's 'Indian middle class'.

In today's conditions, the issue of forcible land acquisition has acquired a very dangerous dimension with the new Agri laws. Legalizing the indiscriminate forcible acquisition of agricultural land, forcibly dispossessing lakhs of farmers, aggravates the agrarian distress even further. The question of land, hence, remains a crucial issue for the Left forces, the most important political force that is today focusing on developing the agrarian struggles against the mounting distress and the neo-liberal policies that are intensifying the process of primitive accumulation of capital.

Linguistic Reorganization

Secondly, the Indian Communists spearheaded the massive popular struggles for the linguistic reorganization of states in independent India. They are thus, among some others, responsible for creating the political 'map' of today's India on reasonably scientific and democratic lines. The struggles for Vishalandhra, Aikya Keralam and Samyukta Maharashtra were led by individuals who later emerged as Communist stalwarts in the country. This paved the way for the integration of the many linguistic nationalities that inhabit India on the basis of equality, in the process of realizing the 'Idea of India'.

Even after the linguistic reorganization of states, many problems and demands of smaller states still remain today, reflecting the lack of equality amongst the various ethnic identities that exist in the country, particularly in the North East. These can only be resolved by ensuring that all the linguistic groups and ethnic national identities are treated equally, with concrete plans backed by finances to tackle the economic backwardness of these areas and giving equal access to all opportunities. It is only the Left that sincerely champions this cause to strengthen the unity and integrity of India.

Secularism

Thirdly, the Communists' steadfast commitment to secularism is based on a recognition of India's reality. It merits repetition that the unity of India with its immense diversity can be maintained only by strengthening the bonds of commonality in this diversity, and not by imposing uniformity upon this diversity like the communal forces currently seek to do. While this is true for all attributes of India's social life, it is of critical importance in relation to religion. Following the Partition of India and its horrendous communal aftermath, secularism became inseparable for realization of the 'Idea of India'. The Indian ruling classes, however, went only halfway in meeting the Communist objective of defining secularism as the separation of religion from politics. This means that while the state protects the individual's choice of faith, it shall not profess or prefer any one religion. In practice, the Indian ruling classes have reduced this to define secularism as equality of all religions. Inherent in this is an inbuilt bias towards the religious faith of the majority. This, in fact, contributes to providing sustenance to the communal and fundamentalist forces.

On this score as well, in today's conditions, it is the Left that remains the most consistent upholder of secularism, spearheading the efforts to forge the broadest people's unity against communalism and the steadfast fight to defend the religious minorities: to ensure their security, safeguarding their identity as equal citizens of our country.

The drawing in of the exploited majority of rural India; the drawing in of the socially oppressed people, especially those who continue to be subjected to obnoxious caste-based oppression and atrocities; the drawing in of the numerous linguistic nationalities; the drawing in of the multi-religious Indian population; and above all, the drawing in of all Indians in an inclusive path of economic and social justice, constituting the core of the inclusionary 'Idea of India', remains an unfulfilled agenda. The struggles for realizing these incomplete tasks constitute the essential agenda of the CPI(M) and the Indian Left. Hence their pivotal role in leading the struggles for realization of the 'Idea of India'.

What Is This RSS Vision?

Two years before the RSS was born, in 1923, V.D. Savarkar published an ideological pamphlet titled *Essentials of Hindutva*. This was re-titled as *Hindutva: Who is a Hindu?* when reprinted subsequently.

The essence of this ideological pamphlet was to define all those, irrespective of their faiths, who consider India to be their *mathrubhumi* (motherland), *pithrubhumi* (fatherland) and *punyabhumi* (holy land), under the ambit of Hindutva. Those who live in India but whose *punyabhumi* is elsewhere, like the Muslims (Mecca and Medina) and the Christians (whose holy land belongs to the currently devastated Palestinian lands of Jerusalem, Bethlehem, etc.), are outside the ambit of Hindutva.

Savarkar further asserted that Hindutva is a political project which has little to do with the Hindu religion. For the establishment of Hindutva, he gave the slogan, 'Hinduize the military, militarize Hindudom' – the inspiration for the current Hindutva campaigns of poisonous hate, violence and terror.

This RSS construct of nationalism is the ideological–theoretical justification for the establishment of its 'Hindu Rashtra' (which is very distanced from Hinduism as a religion and should actually be called '*Hindutva* Rashtra'). This was first articulated by the then *sarsanghchalak* or supreme leader of the RSS, M.S. Golwalkar, in *We, or Our Nationhood Defined*, first published in 1939. This provided the RSS with an ideological formation, not merely in terms of ideas and principles, but also in establishing an organizational structure to achieve the aim of a fascistic 'Hindutva Rashtra'.

This is premised on an assertion of the late RSS chief that 'Hindus have been in undisputed and undisturbed possession of this land for over eight or even ten thousand years before the land was invaded by any foreign race.' And therefore, this land 'came to be known as Hindusthan, the land of the Hindus' (M.S. Golwalkar 1939, p. 6). Historical facts do not bother the RSS. The word 'Hindusthan' was coined by the Arabs to describe lands beyond the River Sindhu (Indus). Those inhabiting these lands were called the 'Hindoos'. (Phonetically, 'S' becomes 'H' in Arabic!)

Hindutva supremacists, having thus 'established' that the Hindus were always and continue to remain a nation on the basis of such an unscientific and ahistorical analysis, proceed to assert the intolerant, theocratic content of such a Hindutva nation:

> The conclusion is unquestionably forced upon us that ... in Hindusthan exists and must needs exist the ancient Hindu nation and nought else but the Hindu Nation. All those not belonging to the national, i.e., Hindu Race, Religion, Culture and Language naturally fall out of the pale of real 'National' life.
>
> Consequently, only those movements are truly 'National' as aim at re-building, re-vitalizing and emancipating from its present stupor, the Hindu Nation. Those only are nationalist patriots, who, with the aspiration to glorify the Hindu race and nation next to

their heart, are prompted into activity and strive to achieve that goal. All others are either traitors and enemies to the National cause, or, to take a charitable view, idiots. (Golwalkar 1939, pp. 43–44)

This is in complete contradiction to the 'Idea of India' as envisaged by the freedom struggle. As Jawaharlal Nehru describes in the *Discovery of India*:

India is an ancient palimpsest on which layer upon layer of thought and reverie had been inscribed, and yet no succeeding layer had completely hidden or erased what had been written previously.

Further, Rabindranath Tagore says: 'Aryans and non-Aryans, Dravidians and Chinese, Scythians, Huns, Pathans and Mongols, all have merged and lost themselves in one body.' And, this body is India.

The RSS project thus constitutes a regression away from realizing the 'Idea of India' as inclusive nationalism. What is being promoted today is an exclusive Hindutva nationalism to establish their fascistic 'Hindu Rashtra'.

The RSS and the Freedom Movement

The role of the Communist freedom fighters is well-documented. All the nine founding members of the CPI(M) Polit Bureau were freedom fighters who spent long years in British jails and subsequently under Congress rule. A.K. Gopalan hoisted the national flag on 15 August 1947 in the Vellore jail, where he was imprisoned by the British. Harkishan Singh Surjeet was arrested when he was a school student as he hoisted the tricolour. The overwhelming majority of the names inscribed in marble at the cellular jail in the Andamans were associated with the Communists and revolutionary groups.

As opposed to this, the RSS was singularly absent; in fact it stayed away from the freedom struggle, focusing on engineering communal conflicts and riots. It has only one claim of a link to the freedom struggle, i.e. V.D. Savarkar. Even this is concocted and engineered.

R.C. Majumdar, an eminent historian of the national movement who was sympathetic to Hindutva tendencies, documents that Savarkar gave a mercy petition to the British on 14 November 1913, seeking his release from the cellular jail in the Andamans. This surrender made him a public ally of the British policy of divide and rule.

In his petition, he assured the British:

> Now no man having the good of India and humanity at heart will blindly step on the thorny paths which in the excited and hopeless situation of India in 1906–1907 beguiled us from the path of peace and progress. Therefore, if the Government in their manifold beneficence and mercy, release me I for one cannot but be the staunchest advocate of constitutional progress and loyalty to the English Government which is the foremost condition of that progress. (Majumdar 1975, pp. 211–13)

Further, in a letter to the British authorities, he wrote:

> I hereby acknowledge that I had a fair trial and just sentence. I heartily abhor methods of violence resorted to in days gone by, and I feel myself duty bound to uphold law and constitution to the best of my powers and am willing to make the reform a success insofar as I may be allowed to do so in future. (From facsimile of the letter published in *Frontline*, 7 April 1995, p. 94)

For the major portion of his life after making peace with the British, his politics was oppositional to the Congress and the Left-led movements rather than the British.

As leader of the Hindu Maha Sabha, he made sure that movements like the Quit India movement of 1942 passed without any participation of members of the Hindu Maha Sabha or the Sanghathanists. He categorically called on the Hindus to give no support to the movement:

> I issue this definite instruction that all Hindu Sanghathanists, in general, holding any post or position of vantage in the government services should stick to them and continue to perform their regular duties. (Amba Prasad, 'The Indian Revolt of 1942', quoted by A.G. Noorani in *Frontline*, 1 December 1995).

In fact, the Bombay Home Department, during the 1942 Quit India movement, observed, 'The Sangh has scrupulously kept itself within the law and in particular has refrained from taking part in the disturbances that broke out in August 1942' (Anderson and Damle 1987).

Even Nanaji Deshmukh, a leading light of the RSS, once raised the question, 'Why did the RSS not take part in the liberation struggle as an organization?' (Deshmukh 1979). Further, throughout the national movement, the RSS always collaborated with the rulers of the princely states who stood in firm opposition to the freedom struggle. One of their closest allies was Raja Hari Singh of Kashmir, who was reluctant to join India.

In order to conceal this reality, they spread canards against the Communists. One need not go into the details of the already richly documented history of the role of the Left in India's struggle for freedom. It would suffice to note that when the country was celebrating the fiftieth anniversary of the Quit India movement, the then President of India, Dr Shankar Dayal Sharma, while addressing the midnight session of the Parliament on 9/10 August, said:

> After large-scale strikes in mills in Kanpur, Jamshedpur and Ahmedabad, a despatch from Delhi dated 5 September 1942, to the Secretary of State, in London, reported about the Communist Party of India: '*the behaviour of many of its members proves what has always been clear, namely, that it is composed of anti-British revolution*'. (Emphasis added)

Partition Horrors

Prime Minister Modi recently announced that the Partition horrors remembrance day, 14 August, will be observed from now on.

Partition of the subcontinent is probably the only instance of such a humongous migration of people. While accurate estimates are perhaps impossible to establish, close to 15 million people crossed the borders – India had then identified 7,295,870 and Pakistan, 7,226,600 displaced people; and between 1 to 2 million people were killed in communal clashes. It was a horrendous experience that continues to fester wounds and prejudices till today. Hindus, Muslims and Sikhs have all suffered.

By choosing Pakistan's Independence Day for this occasion, Prime Minister Modi is giving a message loaded with communal overtones. Clearly, he wants the present generation not to merely recollect the horror, but to actually relive the horror. Otherwise, he could well have chosen 3 June, the day Partition was announced by the British Viceroy Lord Mountbatten.

The intention is obviously to further sharpen communal polarization in order to facilitate the project of transforming the secular–democratic Republic of India into a rabidly intolerant, theocratic, fascistic Hindutva Rashtra.

The Two-Nation Theory
The foundation for the Partition was laid by the 'Two-Nation Theory'. It was V.D. Savarkar who first advanced this theory in its complete sense. In 1937, in his presidential address to the All India Hindu Maha Sabha conference in Karnavati, Ahmedabad, he said, 'India cannot be assumed today to be a unitarian and homogeneous nation, but on the contrary, there are two

nations in the main; the Hindus and the Moslems, in India' (Savarkar 1963–65, p. 296). In March 1939 once again, in his presidential speech at the Hindu Maha Sabha conference, Savarkar declared: 'We Hindus are a nation by ourselves … we Hindus are marked out as an abiding Nation by ourselves" (see *Indian Annual Register*, 1939, vol. II).

Two years later, on 22 March 1940, in his presidential address to the All India Muslim League conference delivered at Lahore, Mohammed Ali Jinnah said,

> To yoke together two such nations under a single state, one as a numerical minority and the other as a majority, must lead to growing discontent and final destruction of any fabric that may be so built for the government of such a state.

Subsequently, Savarkar, endorsing Jinnah, stated, 'I have no quarrel with Mr Jinnah's two-nation theory. We, Hindus, are a nation by ourselves, and it is a historical fact that Hindus and Muslims are two nations' (*Indian Annual Register*, 1943, vol. II).

Thus Savarkar, who is the Sangh Parivar and Modi's pre-eminent leader, pre-dates Jinnah in advancing the two-nation theory that led to the Partition, which the British admirably aided and abetted.

Gandhi Assassination

Noted historian Mridula Mukherjee, in her presidential address to the Indian History Congress in Malda, West Bengal, 2011, said:

On 15 August 1947, two nation-states were born. One of them, Pakistan, could be said to conform to Savarkar's definition of a nation, but the one to which he belonged, India, was stubbornly refusing to fall in line. The biggest obstacle, it seemed, was the Mahatma himself. He had to be removed. With him alive, neither Hindu Rashtra nor Akhand Bharat could become a reality.

There is consensus that it was an extreme wing of the Hindu Maha Sabha led by Savarkar that was behind Gandhiji's murder. In January 1948, when Gandhiji was assassinated, Savarkar was arrested as the mastermind behind the conspiracy. He was eventually exonerated in the Gandhi Murder Trial for lack of evidence to corroborate the testimony of the approver, a technical point of criminal law. Sardar Patel, being a fine criminal lawyer, was personally convinced of Savarkar's guilt; otherwise, he would not have agreed to put him up for trial. He told Jawaharlal Nehru in unambiguous terms, 'It was a fanatical wing of the Hindu Maha Sabha directly under Savarkar that [hatched] the conspiracy and saw it through.'

When the Commission of Inquiry set up in 1965 under Justice Jiwan Lal Kapoor, a former judge of the Supreme Court of India, gave its report, it came to the following conclusion: 'All these facts taken together were destructive of any theory other than the conspiracy to murder by Savarkar and his group.'

RSS Banned

Following the assassination of Mahatma Gandhi, Sardar Vallabhbhai Patel, whom the RSS and the Modi government seek feverishly to coopt into their fold today, banned the RSS. A government communique dated 4 February 1948, drafted by Sardar Patel, announcing the ban on the RSS says:

> The objectionable and harmful activities of the Sangh have, however, continued unabated and the cult of violence sponsored and inspired by the activities of the Sangh has claimed many victims. The latest and the most precious to fall was Gandhiji himself.

Mahatma Gandhi's private secretary Pyarelal, in his book, *Mahatma Gandhi: The Last Phase* (p. 756), recollects:

> A letter which Sardar Patel received after the assassination from a young man, who according to his own statement had been guiled into joining the RSS organization but was later disillusioned, described how members of the RSS at some places had been instructed beforehand to tune in their radio sets on the fateful Friday for the 'good news'. After the news, sweets were distributed in RSS circles at several places, including Delhi.

The ban on the RSS was in effect from 4 February 1948 to 10 July 1949. Eager to negotiate the withdrawal of the ban, the RSS entered into deceitful compromises with the Government of India. It agreed with Sardar Patel to confine itself as a cultural organization and to not be involved in politics. The RSS, thus, needed a political arm under its leadership and control for furthering its political activities. The Hindu Maha Sabha leader Shyama

Prasad Mukherjee, after his resignation from Jawaharlal Nehru's Union Cabinet opposing amendments to the Hindu Code Bill, was seeking to form a separate political party. In 1952, the RSS sent cadres to assist Shyama Prasad Mukherjee to launch the Bharatiya Jan Sangh, whose later incarnation is the present BJP (Basu, Datta, Sarkar, Sarkar and Sen 1993).

The BJP is thus nothing else but the political arm of the RSS, controlling state power and all the important organs of the Indian state. It is now seeking the destruction of the secular–democratic Constitutional Republic, to realize the RSS's political project of establishing a theocratic, fascistic '*Hindutva Rashtra*'. This is the real meaning and content of Modi's 'New India' at 75.

Destruction of the Indian Constitution

Central to the success of the RSS project is the destruction of the present Indian Constitution. The Indian Constitution rests on four foundational pillars, namely – secular democracy, federalism, social justice, economic sovereignty. Each one of these is under a severe assault since 2014, and has intensified post-2019.

Such a severe undermining of the Indian Constitution is taking place through a corporate–communal nexus that has emerged since 2014. This nexus pursues unbridled neo-liberal reforms, looting of national assets, intensifying economic exploitation and social oppression and establishing a unitary state structure – all of which are so essential for the success of the fascistic Hindutva project, with the emergence of crony capitalism of the worst order.

Destruction of Independent Constitutional Institutions

Beginning with the Parliament, the judiciary, the Election Commission, the Central Bureau of Investigation (CBI), Enforcement Directorate (ED) and all other institutions established by the Constitution to function as checks and balances in our system are being systematically undermined.

The Central Committee of the CPI(M) has been regularly analysing these developments alongside the ruination of the lives and livelihoods of the people. The assaults on secularism and on constitutionally guaranteed democratic rights and civil liberties of the people are on the rise.

The utter mismanagement of the Covid pandemic and the vaccine shortages, along with woeful public health facilities, continue to take their toll on peoples' lives. Unconcerned about all this in the most callous manner, this government singlemindedly pursues its fascistic project under the slogan of 'new India'. It employs the necessary means to achieve this objective. An important aspect of this is to control people's lives.

Surveillance State

In the last seven years, surveillance of citizens, violating the fundamental rights guaranteed by the Indian Constitution to personal privacy, has sharply escalated.

The collection of biometric data forcibly and without individual concurrence, through Aadhar, Universal Health Identification, etc., is an assault on peoples' privacy, providing information for the consolidation of a surveillance state.

The exposures concerning the use by the Modi government of the notorious Israeli Pegasus military-grade spyware on individuals is an ominous fascistic trend. This is not only a violation of personal privacy, but constitutes an attack on Indian democracy itself. Among those whose mobile phones were/are under surveillance are political leaders, a former judge of the Supreme Court the bureaucracy, the judiciary, a former member of the Election Commission, former director of the CBI, and several media personalities who are courageous to tell the people the truth, amongst others, i.e. all the independent institutions of our democracy. The timing of such surveillance is also ominous, as it came on the eve of the 2019 general elections.

Promoting Irrationalism: Destroying Reason

For the regressive project of 'Hindutva Rashtra' to succeed in India, the RSS/BJP's effort to influence and control peoples' social consciousness is central. This requires promoting irrationality and unreason, and replacing history with Hindu mythology and philosophy with Hindu theology. The BJP government is systematically reworking the syllabus taught to our students and youth, attacking and seeking to neutralize universities that nurture rationalism and scientific enquiry, and appointing Hindutva ideologues to various positions in higher education.

At a philosophical level, they seek to resurrect irrationalism as the mainstay for the success of this pernicious project. Georg Lukacs' seminal work, *Destruction of Reason,* in the form of a critique of philosophical irrationalism, needs to be recollected in our Indian context today. Lukacs traces, amongst others, Germany's path to Hitler in the realm of philosophy. He was particularly concerned about this, as it had been Germany that provided the world with an enlightened rationalist philosophy in the nineteenth century. Hegelian dialectics and Karl Marx's work to make Hegel, who was 'standing on his head to stand on his feet', was the philosophical legacy of the German people. How could they, then, internalize the irrational philosophy of Nazism? Lukacs' central contention asserts 'irrationalism as an international phenomenon in the imperialist world'.

Irrationalism, by its very definition, is an ideological trend hostile to reason. Its main objective in all its manifestations, from the days of the European Enlightenment to today's imperialist globalization, is to challenge the power of reason in human affairs and its capacity to provide knowledge about reality. Knowledge, at any point in time, can never explain the whole reality. However, irrationalism negates the dialectical relationship between reality and knowledge. Objective reality is, as Lukacs says, far richer and more complex than our knowledge of it. Instead of seeking to bridge this gap on the basis of rationality by pursuing a dialectical method to scientifically comprehend reality, irrationalism concludes that 'one cannot obtain rational knowledge of the entire reality'. The entire reality can only be grasped with 'faith' or 'intuition', considered a higher form of knowledge. Hindutva nationalism feeds people with such 'faith', and thus feeds itself, to promote its twin objectives of furthering the neo-liberal agenda and transforming India into an exclusivist, theocratic, fascistic state.

The methodology adopted currently by the RSS–BJP–Modi combine to consolidate the hold of this 'false consciousness' of Hindutva nationalism is to ensure that objective facts are less influential in shaping public opinion than appeals to emotion and personal belief.

By controlling the media and social media, emotional appeals and the building up of a personality cult continuously bombard us with propaganda that India is prospering in a hitherto unknown manner, and the only obstacles in the creation of an Indian *El Dorado* are the Muslims, the Christians and the Communists.

By creating a make-believe world in which the people are forced to live and battle with issues based on emotional appeals totally divorced from the miseries of their day-to-day existence, they seek to divert the people's attention away from the struggles against intensified exploitation and oppression.

It is such philosophical irrationalism that permeates all aspects of India's socio-political-cultural life under this RSS–BJP government today. This is, simply put, Unreason.

Conclusion

This is the holistic manner in which the Indian Constitution, our Republic and the 'Idea of India' are being destroyed. An equally holistic counter-effort has to be mounted to first save and then strengthen the secular–democratic Indian Republic. All spheres – political, ideological, social, cultural – must be encompassed in order to erect the counter-hegemony against this fascistic Hindutva hegemony that is being rapidly erected.

Marx and Engels, in *German Ideology*, explained how the ideas of the ruling classes are the ruling ideas of their age. Gramsci analysed and explained how the hegemony of ruling ideas is not enforced merely by the state and its institutions. The state is only the 'outer ditch', behind which stands a powerful system of 'fortresses and earthworks', and a network of cultural institutions and values which buttress the domination of the ruling classes with their ideas.

This hegemony is mediated and transmitted through a complex web of social relations and the consequent social structures. The family, the community, caste, religion, its places of worship and its festivals, various forms of cultural expression like theatre, cinema, television, social media programmes, are the modes that constantly feed the fodder to shape values and opinions, fostering the Hindutva hegemony of 'ideas'. In the process, they create the 'myth' of a 'common culture'. This 'common culture' is nothing but the selective transmission of Hindutva, its ideas and its values being passed off as 'common sense'.

The creation of the crucial counter-hegemony over society through the creation of a new culture embraces both class struggle against the relations of production, economic exploitation and associated political activity, and struggles in the realm of civil society against the efforts that transmit and strengthen the hold and hegemony of Hindutva.

The counter-hegemony must be based on strengthening the basic struggles of the working people, our peasantry, our women, Dalits, Adivasis, youth, students, etc., against the policies of class exploitation. This is the foundation on which must be built our advance, to achieve our revolutionary goal of People's Democracy in the march towards Socialism.

On the strength of these struggles, a larger unity with the likes of sections of society that came together in our epic freedom struggle needs to be built, to save India today in order to change it for a better tomorrow.

The choice before us in India at 75 is between taking India into the backwardness and darkness of its medieval past, hailed by Hindutva as the 'glory of Hindu civilization', or taking it into the brightness of the future as a modern, forward-looking, world-influencing Republic.

References

Anderson, Walter K. and Damle, Sridhar D., *The Brotherhood in Saffron: The Rashtriya Swayamsevak Sangh and Hindu Revivalism,* New Delhi: Vistaar Publications, 1987.

Basu, Tapan, Datta, Pradip, Sarkar, Sumit, Sarkar, Tanika and Sen, Sambuddha, *Khaki Shorts: Saffron Flags,* Tracts for the Times/1, Delhi: Orient Longman, 1993.

Bilgrami, Akeel, 'Introduction', *Social Scientist*, Vol. 39, No. 1–2, January–February 2011, pp. 1–10.

Deshmukh, Nana, *R.S.S.: Victim of Slander*, New Delhi: Vision Books, 1979.

Golwalkar, M.S., *We or Our Nationhood Defined*, with a foreword by Loknayak M.S. Aney, Bharat Publications: 1, 1939.

Majumdar, R.C., *Penal Settlement in Andamans*, Department of Culture, Government of India, 1975.

Prasad, Amba, 'India's Revolt of 1942', dissertation, Department of History, Stanford University, 1952.

Pyarelal, *Mahatma Gandhi: The Last Phase*, 3 vols, Ahmedabad: Navajivan Publishing House, 1956.

Savarkar, V.D., *Samagra Savarkar Vadmay*, Volume 6, Maharashtra Prantik Hindu Sabha Publication, 1963–65.

First published in Marxist, *vol. XXXVII, no. 1–2, January–June 2021.*